Book 4

RESISTING NAZI OCCUPATION

**The Dutch in Wartime
Survivors Remember**

Edited by

Anne van Arragon Hutten

D1235614

Mokeham Publishing Inc.

P.O. Box 35026, Oakville, Ontario, L6L 0C8, Canada
P.O. Box 559, Niagara Falls, New York, 14304, USA
www.mokeham.com

Cover photograph by Hein Bijvoet

ISBN 978-0-9868308-5-3

Contents

On the front cover

The Dockworker commemorates the bravery of the workers of Amsterdam and surrounding areas who went on strike in support of their maltreated Jewish compatriots in February of 1941. The February Strike was one of the first organized acts of resistance by the Dutch, and resulted in brutal oppression by the Nazi regime.

The statue was created by Haarlem sculptor Mari Andriessen and unveiled by Queen Juliana in 1952. It was placed in the centre of Amsterdam's Jewish district - at the time virtually deserted after the Holocaust.

The monument depicts a labourer, strong arms held wide in a gesture that shows both a desire to fight back and an offer to protect. The statue symbolizes how ordinary everyday people called upon hitherto undiscovered inner strength in their fight against the oppressor.

An annual commemoration ceremony takes place at the statue on February 25.

Introduction

Anne van Arragon Hutten

As was noted in the previous three books in this series, we are publishing the wartime memories of ordinary Dutch citizens. Despite the hundreds of books already written about the war, the stories continue to pour out. The impact of World War ll was so traumatizing that anyone who lived through it continues to feel its effects even into the 21st century.

My grandchildren all know that 'Grammy was born in the war'. I was only four when the war ended, and nevertheless it has strongly influenced the person I have become. No doubt those who were teenagers or adults at the time will have far more personal war memories to share, but the war affected everyone, even the unborn and the infants of that time. I have spoken with other Dutch-Canadian immigrant women who, like me, really dislike working at a community supper where so many leftovers have to be thrown out. We are too aware that food is a vital resource. Wasting food feels like a sin, not just because it was so scarce during that war, but because millions of people today still go hungry.

If some of us tend to be unusually intense and serious, it is because so early on we sensed the fear and insecurity of living under a deeply evil regime. Life isn't all fun; shallow pleasures are fleeting. Actually, life itself is fleeting, here today and gone tomorrow. That was a hard-learned lesson of World War ll, and even those of us too young to understand it absorbed it into the marrow of our bones. The sound of endless waves of bombers passing overhead during the night in that last winter of war drove home the message: be afraid, because that bomb can fall on you.

It may not have been that way for everyone. As was demonstrated, particularly immediately after the war, many – mostly young – people went overboard in their search for freedom and fun. Many tried to live in a lighthearted spirit, enjoying life while they had it. Why waste time thinking about death and destruction? Behind that outlook I still detect the war: let's enjoy life while it lasts.

Most ordinary Dutch people probably had little time for such thoughts while they coped with an irrational enemy whose cruelty seemed limitless. Some found it easier to just go with the flow. If Germany was all-powerful, why resist? Might as well do as they say, and even work with them to keep our stubborn neighbours in line. There were plenty who collaborated with the enemy, betraying the young man hiding next door, or the visiting blonde 'niece from Amsterdam' with the dark hair roots.

A large majority of those ordinary wartime people refused to travel that traitorous route. The Dutch, as a people, have long valued freedom of speech, of religion, of choice. They were not going to roll over and play dead as the Nazi war machine rolled over them. In many small ways they resisted, whether by burying their copper pans in the back yard or by hiding one or more young men in their homes to protect them from slave labour.

It is their stories we want to tell in this book.

Historical background

The Dutch Resistance movement during World War ll consisted of many individuals and small groups, working under cover of their legitimate careers, or under cover of darkness, often with false identity papers.

Soon after the Germans invaded the Netherlands, various organizations sprang up to protest the blanket propaganda, the sly insinuation that the Germans and Dutch were all Aryans, and thus all on the same side.

In February of 1941 a strike broke out in Amsterdam and surrounding areas to protest the singling out of Jews for exclusion from many careers and public places, and the first violent round-ups of Jews. Students went on strike that same year, as did metalworkers who hated to see their work support the enemy's war effort.

Eighteen prisoners were executed on March 13, 1941 for working against the occupiers. These included organizers of the February Strike and members of a group that had published chain letters and pamphlets calling on Dutch citizens to reject German orders and doctrine. These men had all operated fairly openly, without much consideration for secrecy and security. The mass killing shocked many Dutch into recognizing the true character of the Nazi regime. From then on the Resistance movement went underground.

By the end of 1941, various organizations had started to produce and distribute illegal newsletters and newspapers to keep the Dutch people informed about what was really happening, with other media firmly under German control.

Late in 1942, several small resistance groups were combined to form a national organization to help those who had gone into hiding for any reason. This group was notable for being unarmed. They included people from all walks of life. At first it was mainly the Jews who had to be hidden and protected, but as the war went on, more and more people found their life to be in danger. Very often these were the young men who, according to German demands, should have meekly lined up at the curb to wait for transportation to Germany. Not being on the official population rolls any longer, those in hiding no longer received ration coupons for food and other necessities. These now had to be supplied somehow.

Other groups did take up arms. They robbed distribution centers for those necessary ration coupons. They also raided prisons to free captured Resistance workers. As the war progressed more people went into hiding and it became necessary to feed them somehow. According to most estimates, between 300,000 and 350,000 people were forced to go into hiding, especially after participating in a number of strikes that were unsuccessful in stopping the occupiers. In April and May of 1943, spontaneous strikes erupted over the threatened imprisonment or forced labour of Holland's former military personnel.

It was largely these latter strikes, ongoing over a two-month period, that finally convinced the German leadership they would never win the hearts and minds of the Dutch, and their restrictive measures became ever more severe. The railroad strike in September of 1944 not only failed to lift the heavy hand of the oppressors, but also caused them to actively blockade food supplies to the cities.

In each case, organizers of these strikes were in mortal danger, and very many of them went underground. It was often the Resistance organizations which found them a new place to live, supplied them with ration coupons, moved them to a new location when danger threatened, or even freed them from jail after their capture.

Dutchmen who collaborated with the Germans sometimes managed to infiltrate a Resistance group, and would then betray everyone involved. The result was imprisonment, usually torture, and often death.

As the war progressed, the occupation continued, and the regime became ever more brutal, organized resistance grew. Resistance members were involved in the hiding of Allied pilots who had parachuted from their stricken aircraft, and who then had to be smuggled back to London. They moved Jewish people of all ages from place to place as danger threatened. They blew up bridges and railroad tracks to slow down the Germans. In a few cases they deliberated together before executing a collaborator, when it was necessary to prevent the betrayal of Resistance groups. They gathered local information on the movement of German troops and communicated this to England via illegal radio systems. Couriers, often girls and young women transported underground newsletters from place to place; they hid the clandestine materials in the frame of their bicycle or under their clothing. Those who did have to work for Germany at gunpoint tried hard to sabotage whatever they were making.

On September 5, 1944, various Resistance groups, which until then had worked largely independently of each other, formally joined forces to form the

Binnenlandse Strijdkrachten (BS), or Inland Forces. Although the BS went largely unarmed at first, after clandestine radio contact between London and the BS-command in Holland, British planes secretly started parachuting weapons in the dead of night. Resistance fighters had to guide the planes to the right field with beacons, at night, while a curfew was in place. It was extremely risky to attend these night-drops and retrieve the parachuted crates.

Resistance against the regime did not always take on an organized form. Many people resisted in their own way. They held on to radios, copper or bicycles that should have been handed in to the German authorities. They listened to the BBC and read and passed on underground newsletters. They went into hiding instead of volunteering for work in Germany. Even these acts of defiance, which may seem minor to us now when compared to active armed resistance, carried a real risk of severe reprisal.

Estimates vary wildly, and depend partially on how one defines 'resistance', but there is no doubt that many thousands (one estimate goes as high as 25,000) lost their life resisting the Nazis in The Netherlands.

Razzia

A razzia was a German World War II practice used in occupied countries, whereby German police or military rounded up civilians on the streets of towns and cities. The civilians were sometimes specifically targeted groups, sometimes random passers-by. Those caught in a razzia were either taken hostage, drafted for war work, sent to prisons or concentration camps, or summarily executed.

My father had a Gestetner

Hans Hofenk (aka 'Hans van der Kooi' for four months)

When Germany occupied Holland during World War ll, life changed for everyone. I remember those years well, and would like to share some of my memories from when I was a child in a Mennonite family.

The war started on May 10, 1940, a week before my birthday. It was announced on the radio that German soldiers had crossed the border and that fighting between the Dutch and German armies had begun. All schools were closed immediately for the duration of the fighting, and for a ten-year-old, that was okay.

When Germany had invaded Poland earlier, they had bombed Warsaw in order to obtain capitulation of the Polish government. Similarly, the bombing of Rotterdam forced the Dutch government to surrender. Military strategy has been, for centuries, to kill the civilian population to win wars.

The Germans were soon everywhere in Holland and needed quarters to live in. Thus lots of schools suddenly housed military personnel. The school I attended was a fairly new one, and we had to share with another school. One week we had classes in the morning, and the following week in the afternoon.

The Germans controlled all aspects of life. The broadcasting of news was subject to German approval. They even changed history: I remember that sections of the school history books, unfriendly to the Germans, were taped over by the teachers. Needless to say we

11

soon found a way to read the forbidden passages. Food became scarce and ration cards were issued. Jewish children could no longer attend public schools and Jews were forced to wear the yellow star at all times.

An 'Underground movement' started, initially to provide impartial news but later to help people hiding from the Germans find lodging. My father had a Gestetner, a duplicating machine which was used to produce one-page newsletters. However, it was soon too dangerous to have such equipment in the house, so the Gestetner was moved to a secret location. If the Germans caught a producer, distributor or reader of one of these papers they would be sent to prison.

All men between 18 and 45 had to register so they could be sent to Germany to replace German workers who had gone to the battle front. My brother, who was eighteen when the war broke out, was allowed to finish high school and work for some months before he was called to work in Germany He decided to go into hiding rather than work for the Germans. He didn't come out of hiding until May 4, 1945. One of my friend's brothers had gone to Germany and during an air raid on the factory where he was working, escaped and made his way back to Holland. A little later his parents received notice that their son had been killed during an Allied attack, and if they wanted his remains they should forward some money. They did that, of course.

Events like that put pressure on the Underground to find lodging for the people that wanted to go into hiding instead of working in Germany. This got much worse in September, 1944, after the Battle of Arnhem. The Allied forces had freed the southern part of Holland! Railroad workers were asked to go on strike so that the Germans could not use the railway system for transporting their military supplies. Hundreds and hundreds of railroad workers and their families were forced to leave their homes and go into hiding. They had to be relocated, supplied with false identity papers, ration cards, and other necessities.

Because of the railroad strike and the lack of telephone connections, communication between the various Resistance organizations became very difficult. Our home, located in the center of the city and having a store on the main floor, became an exchange post where couriers, usually girls or young women, could drop off parcels with information, and pick up replies. Some came from the large cities and had biked over sixty miles. They had to have our address, of course, and that was dangerous for us and our families.

During October of that year, my father had pneumonia, and while our family doctor was visiting him the phone rang. The doctor, poor fellow, had probably not heard a phone ring for a couple of years and he jumped. He was a customer on my paper route and we knew that we could trust him. When the Resistance people told us that Dad would be picked up for interrogation that night, the doctor suggested that we should move him. Which is what we did. My mother, sister and I burned as much incriminating material as we could find. I still delivered some papers before curfew at 8 p.m. and then we went to bed.

That night they came, searched the house, and took my mother to the local jail. My sister and I could not sleep anymore and we discussed what we should do. One thing was to clear the house of all food items, precious belongings and clothes because we could not stay there.

The local jail was an impressive three-storey building built like a fort, with a moat around it. My mother was in a cell with other women, two of them couriers. In another part of this jail were two of the Resistance leaders who had been 'interrogated' several times and could break down at any time. That would cause hundreds of people to be picked up for illegal activities. It was imperative that they be freed from jail.

On December 8, the Resistance was able to get fifty political prisoners out. Thanks to careful planning it took only one hour to get everybody out and into a hiding place before 8 p.m. when no one was allowed to be out in the street.

The next morning the city buzzed with all kinds of stories: that the prisoners had been moved by ambulances to the outside of the city, and other tales. In fact all of them had been housed in hiding places within the city, and none of them, nor any of the liberators, was caught. They were all provided with a new name, picture identification, and other necessities.

My sister and I were told by the Resistance to leave the city immediately. We were provided with a bike and were on our way within an hour to join our brother who was hiding on a farm thirty miles away. He was shocked to see us, since he had not known that Mom had been jailed.

On Saturday, December 23, a stranger on a bike rode up the farm's almost mile-long driveway. He looked somewhat familiar. He had a mustache, wore wooden shoes, and had on a funny sailor's cap. Since one never knew who might come up the driveway, my brother and two others were already in their hiding places when we recognized Dad. He had hoped that we would be on that farm. That night the farmer found a bed for him too.

On Christmas Eve a lady rode up the driveway and sure enough, she was our mother. She had biked about forty miles that frosty day. It was a long evening before we all went to bed.

A few days later another visitor came to tell us that having five members of one family in one hiding place was too many. As a result, my sister Truus and I were sent to a widow with three unmarried daughters, and my parents were moved to a young couple not too far away from us. We stayed there until early May when the Canadian army liberated our hometown.

How did we feel about the Germans after the war?

In 1946, my mother accepted a boarder, a young girl from Essen, Germany, whose house had been bombed. She stayed with us for six months and shared our still meagre food supplies.

In 1948 I went to Germany with the Mennonite Central Committee to help rebuild an old castle as a refugee center for German refugees.

They sent him to Vught

Jacoba Robbertsen

We experienced a lot of misery. There was an air raid shelter for all the people in our street. Whenever the siren went off, we quickly had to go into the shelter and stay there until the all clear was given.

My brother was the right age to be sent to Germany for forced labour, but he didn't go. He went into hiding instead and helped the Resistance. Two cousins were sent to Germany, but after some time they had enough of that and wandered back home, with all the problems that entailed. So of course they had to go into hiding too, with our Van de Loosdrecht grandparents.

My uncle, Jos van de Loosdrecht, had joined the underground movement right away when the war broke out. When the war was nearly over, the SS caught him and sent him to Vught Concentration Camp. They lined him up with a bunch of other men and shot them all.

Dad in his long johns

Pieter Koeleman

When war broke out we were a family of six living in Noordwijk, a village on the North Sea coast. We were regularly confronted with restrictions and other limitations. We were used to going to the beach or to the dunes with the family, but ever more areas became prohibited terrain. Like most people we learned what it meant to be hungry and afraid.

We all had to do our part in the household. One of the tasks I had was to keep the heat going. In our neighbourhood we had a gasworks. We regularly went to the area where the coal waste was dumped in order to try and find small bits of coal that could still be used. At other times we walked along a narrow asphalt road to the dunes, where, along the bottom edge, small birch trees grew. With a small axe or handsaw, both dull, together with other boys from our street, we tried to chip or saw through the green wood.

Close by, there was an institute for mentally handicapped children. Shortly after the war started, the children had been evacuated to an inland town and the Germans now occupied the institute. The whole area was restricted, and it was patrolled regularly. We had to hide if we were there during a patrol, but it happened more than once that we were discovered and had to run to escape. This meant having to leave our wood treasures behind and coming home with empty hands and wet pants.

One time my oldest brother and I went to a different area with the same assignment: get some wood for the stove. Pulling the frame of a baby carriage, we walked to the northern part of the village. We were not alone, as other kids too were trying to cut down some small trees. The weather deteriorated and soon it started to rain. The lightning and thunder were terrifying. We loaded up what we had and ran with our carriage along the dirt path to the road. We were getting scared and as it would take such a long time to get home, we decided to dump our trees in the ditch behind a privet hedge and go back for them the next morning.

The next day we returned to pick up our loot, but it was gone. We had a good idea who had stolen our wood, and walked to a house close by where a boy nicknamed 'Pete the Shit' lived. The small backyard had a wall and gate, which was locked. Peeking over the wall from the backyard we saw our small stems. We shouted: "come out, we know you are there. It's ours." There was no response, and, very disappointed, we walked home, empty handed once more.

One evening I heard my dad talking to my older brother, planning to go to an area with the name 'Finch Field' not that far from where we lived. My dad would not allow me to go with them. They used the same undercarriage and a different, two-person, saw, which they could use for larger logs. There were no trees in the field, just telephone poles. It took quite a while to cut down a pole and they moved it to the edge of the road. With dawn coming my dad left because he was on the Germans' wanted list and did not want to get caught. It was up to my brother to see how he could get the pole home. He made it but it there was not much left of the pram's undercarriage as the weight of the pole had crushed the whole frame.

Dad had a one man carrier company. Regularly he was forced to drive for the Germans. This caused frightening hours for our family at night waiting for when, or if, he would come home. One time he came in the room still with his coat on and with a kind of strange smile. Why don't you take your coat off, my mother asked. He kept that mysterious smile. Then he opened his coat and a small suckling pig jumped out of it onto the floor. Hilarity all over, as we boys were trying to catch that screaming pink creature. Finally my dad could bring our new family member to a sty in the shed. That was one of our rare moments of fun.

It was in the beginning of 1944 that in the middle of the night an enormous noise could be heard in our street. A raid started with the Germans searching for men and older boys. Mom and dad were sleeping in the front room on the second floor, the two girls on the landing and we, the three boys, in the bedroom at the back. We lived in an old farmhouse and our bedroom door was always open. Against the door stood a three-cornered chair with a thatched seat. When the noise started all of a sudden we saw my dad, dressed in a white undershirt and long johns, jump on the chair, push the lid of the loft away, step on the edge of the backrest and gone he was. The lid was back in place. In the meantime the Germans were banging on our front door with their rifle butts.

"*Aufmachen*, open up," they shouted.

"Yes, I am coming, yes, I am coming", my mother repeated while she carefully went down the steep stairs. She was eight months pregnant with her sixth child. The banging went on and mom was now responding in German: "*Ja, ja, ich komme,*" hoping that that would help. She opened the door with her impressive belly blocking the entrance of the hallway. The jerks pushed her roughly out of their way and snarled repeatedly, "Where is your husband?" while searching the main floor.

"He is driving for you Germans," Mom answered firmly. We were all listening breathlessly to the noise downstairs and especially to what Mom was saying and if she was all right. Finally they left and the noise gradually subsided as they moved down the street. After a while my Dad appeared again in his long johns and we all sighed with relief. Nobody had much sleep for the rest of that night. It occurred to me later that I would never again see such unusual athletic activity from my dad.

Only bad people went to jail

Elizabeth Gilbert-de Graaff

I was born in Laren, North Holland, and was almost six years old when the war broke out. My first memory of the war is that German soldiers took over our school, the Maria Montessori School. The teachers gave each child some school supplies to take home, and I took stuff I needed for Grade One arithmetic. We had to keep that at home until the school would be available again.

My father was in jail, in Amsterdam, for six weeks. I couldn't understand that at all, because only bad people went to jail. The neighbours brought us food and were nice to Mom, so I thought maybe Dad wasn't all bad or they wouldn't do that. It seems he had done something for the Jews, on behalf of the Resistance movement and the Germans had been watching him. However, because they had no real proof they let him go again.

One time the Germans needed blankets and went from house to house. Each family had to donate one blanket. Mom gave them the thinnest blanket she could find.

Another time they needed men, so they blocked all the streets in town, and picked up every man they saw. My father heard about it, so he fled town. As he was hiding under a pile of cut brush a solder walked in his direction. Dad thought he had been found, but the soldier just had to pee and then left again. That was a relief for Dad!

Germany needed leather and so we never got new shoes. The man who made wooden shoes in town was very busy keeping the children supplied. I remember

21

watching him at work, just to see how he made them. All the children wore wooden shoes; grownups, I don't remember.

Too risky to trust anyone

Afine Relk

The second year of the war we found out that some of our neighbours, and even family members, had joined the NSB. Many of them worked for the Nazis. These people were nothing but losers and traitors who thought they would be better off siding with the Germans. They supplied the Germans with names and addresses of their neighbours who were against the Germans,

We were told to bring every copper or brass item we owned to a collection point in the city, from where it was sent to the factories in Germany to make bullets and other weapons. Of course we brought as little as possible, and buried our belongings in the back yard.

It was too dangerous to trust anyone. Little kids, and older ones too, were never told anything that was going on because it was just too risky; they might give out the information unwittingly. At night when we were in bed, the radio was taken out of its hiding place under the house's threshold, and the grownups listened to the BBC broadcast from England. Sometimes Queen Wilhelmina would give encouraging messages.

I have several Dutch friends who hid downed pilots in their orchards or on their farms, and who were later sponsored to come to America by those same American pilots. Another friend, when he was seventeen, saved a pilot by lying to the Germans. He had learned German in high school, so he could communicate with them and lie about the pilot's whereabouts. Eventually the

Germans determined that he had lied to them. They tied him to a telephone pole with a piece of wire that seriously injured his voice box, and he has had trouble speaking ever since.

Yet another friend's father was hiding ammunition and resistance men on his farm, and the NSB betrayed him. The Germans shot the father and grandfather, and made the wife watch it. Then they burned down the farm.

Towards the end of the war, we heard the Allied bombers going overhead towards Germany, and coming back a couple of hours later. We saw the searchlights in the dunes where the Germans were trying to shoot down the planes.

How we escaped to England

Tony Stroeve

Everything really started with my first attempt to escape to England via France and Spain. This was early in 1943 and three of us, all schoolmates from a Maritime college, were to join a small group at the station to catch the train to Paris. The only other person who knew about this escapade was Chris de Bakker, another schoolmate. While we were waiting on the platform for the train to arrive, Chris came rushing over to our group and told us to forget about the trip as the whole thing was a set-up and we would finish up in Germany as slave labour. Two of the fellows would not believe Chris and got on the train just the same, while I took his word and went back home. I never heard from the other chaps again.

Two months later, I received a phone call from Chris asking me if I was still interested in going to England. If so, there was a place available on a boat leaving within weeks. Of course I jumped at the chance of getting away as it was getting pretty risky being seen on the street, the Germans having the nasty habit of now and then picking up any able-bodied male and sending them straight to Germany. This time I had to tell my Mother what was going on. I do not think that she was very happy with the idea.

In April, Chris and I met in The Hague at the house of another chap going on the journey. There were ten of us, including the lady of the house and her daughter, so sleeping quarters were quite cramped. For four weeks, the eight of us had to sleep in the front room on mattresses. We were not allowed to make much noise, as the neighbours were not supposed to know that so many people lived at that address. Food being rationed, each of us had to hand over his ration coupons because the women were doing the cooking. As we were not allowed to go out too often, we had plenty of time on our hands and the women put us to work around the house. Everybody was cleaning, washing, ironing, washing up and helping with the cooking.

Just imagine eight healthy young fellows living almost all day in the house, with not much entertainment, only keeping occupied with piddly little things, and the food not being the best either. The cheapest and most filling food available was potatoes, cabbage, Brussels sprouts and pumpkin. The bread, which we had to buy on the black market, was made from daffodil bulbs (we called them trumpet bulbs because they produced an enormous lot of wind), and was as heavy as a brick, very hard to cut and very coarse. Meat being very rare, we bought mince all the time, horse meat of course, giving you more for your coupons than beef or pork.

At last the time of our departure arrived. The takeoff place was somewhere in the southern part of Holland which had to be reached by train and bus. In pairs or alone, we made our way there. A large barge was waiting for us at a wharf. The hold of the boat was completely filled by a smaller boat that was to take us across. We could not get on board before nightfall as it would look suspicious to see eight men getting on board a barge that, under normal circumstances, had a crew of one.

Darkness fell around six o'clock and when the boys got

on board the barge we still had to wait till about eleven o'clock before we could pole the boat away from the shore as the engine could not be used till we were well away from the little town. Inland rivers in the south are not very deep and with four of us poling the boat it did not take very long. Halfway down to the river mouth the skipper killed the engine and anchored the barge. Our little boat was hoisted out of the hold with the boom. It did not take long before the eight of us were settled in it as best we could, finding out how small the boat really was.

She was only eleven feet long, and four feet of that was taken up by the engine, not leaving us very much room to move around in. The barge towed us slowly downriver. A couple of miles from the river's mouth, the skipper let us go, wishing us the best of luck. We floated down stream on the outgoing tide. Getting close to the river mouth we started the engine, which caught promptly, accelerated, coughed, sputtered and belched and then just died. However hard we tried to start the blasted thing, nothing worked, not even the combined swearing and cursing of the whole crew. While this was going on, the boat slowly drifted downstream towards the open sea. Luckily one of the fellows had the sense to throw out the anchor, stopping us from being swept out to sea with no power at all. We kept trying for another half an hour but finally gave up.

We ended up physically towing the boat back to the barge with great difficulty, and got there at four in the morning. The whole thing had been organized by a man named Ton Schrader, so we phoned to tell him the bad news. As it turned out, by the end of the next day the weather had turned so bad that our little boat would have been swamped by the first big wave and the lot of us would probably have drowned, as we did not carry life jackets.

We all had to go back to the old house and be prepared to spend some more time there. The mother and daughter had been told that we were coming back, which was a good thing because the mother's son was one of the crew members in this boat. Every one of the crew members had to let their people know as well that this trip had to be aborted. We had to do this because our crew had a code to be sent out over Radio Orange in England to let family members know that we had made it safely across, otherwise they would have been listening to the clandestine radio messages for months on end not knowing what was going on.

The second escape plan was made about three weeks later. Meanwhile, the crew had increased to eleven men. One of them was a radio operator from New Zealand, who had been shot down over Holland on the 26th of April. He happened to parachute right on top of a greenhouse, going right through it, of course. This was just at the house of one of our crew members. He could not have picked a better spot.

On the 5th of May, we made our second attempt. This time the boat was an eighteen foot monster, giving us more room to move. It was too big to go into the hold of the barge and had to be towed. The skipper had the proper papers as well, supplied through Ton Schrader again. Because of the tide, the boat had to leave the river mouth not later than eleven o'clock that night. It was a moonless night and there was an easterly wind, just right for us.

At ten, everybody got on board our boat and after a quiet "good luck!" from the skipper we shoved off and drifted downstream. After a few minutes, we started the engine, which kept going this time, and under low power we kept the noise to a minimum, not knowing if there were any patrols about. Within ten minutes we were in trouble. With the slow speed, it was very difficult to steer the boat, as there was not enough pressure on the rudder. The tide carried us straight onto a sandbank. Thanks to the slow speed, we were not pushed too far onto the bank and when Chris and I jumped into the water it did not take much effort to push her back into the current again. In all the excitement and panic the two of us never felt the cold water.

To prevent this from happening again, we had to increase speed despite the risk inherent in making more noise. By this time we were getting close to the open sea and started to feel a slight swell which the boat took very well. Putting on more power made the nose come up, and the boat was taking the swell with no bother at all. What did give us a shock was the appearance of a German patrol boat crossing our bow and going North at a greater speed than we were doing. When we saw this we turned South and increased our speed at the same time. This must have been heard by the Germans because they switched on their searchlight and started looking for us. Luckily they kept looking in the direction of the coast, giving us a chance and the time to put more distance between them and us.

They did not keep it up for very long, realizing probably that they were exposing themselves with all that light and were sitting ducks for possible enemy attack. When the searchlight went out, all we could see was the fluorescence of our wake.

The excitement gone, everybody settled down and then we noticed that with the speed we were doing, the bow was taking a pounding which she could not take for very long. We reduced speed and the swell became more noticeable, with the result that a few of the fellows were getting a bit squeamish and it was not long after that, that the first load of vomit was deposited right inside the boat, to everybody's dismay.

We had decided not to attract any attention until we could see the English coast in the distance. One of the boys noticed that there was quite a bit of water in the bilges, which meant of course that we had a leak somewhere. The result was reducing speed again and every one taking a turn at bailing out the water. With daylight coming on, the lookout noticed three small boats approaching from the south. They were going so fast that they must have been either German *Schnellbooten* (speedboats) or English Motor Torpedo Boats. Not wanting to risk it, we slowed down completely and let them go on their way while hoping not to be seen by them. Waiting till they were out of sight, we put on speed again, still going westward.

It was proper daylight now and all of us were wide awake and keeping a look out for anything at all. Around ten o'clock a whole bunch of ships appeared on the horizon, travelling north. This could only be an Allied convoy, and it was at least an hour before they were close enough to see us. We knew that they had seen us, as the ship's railing was full of crew members having a peep at us.

At the end of the convoy, one of the two destroyers

turned our way and slowed down, threw us a line and lowered a rope ladder. As soon as we hit the deck we were surrounded by armed sailors who took us below decks and herded us into a wardroom. Not long after, they came back and supplied us with bread, butter, cheese and a pot of strong tea. When they left, they took the New Zealnder with them and we did not see him again till later that night at the railway station in the port town of Harwich under escort of two Air Force military. When he saw us he came over. We were the best people he ever met, etc. After that, we never saw him again.

After hours on the destroyer, we at last entered Harwich harbour, where the harbour police escorted us into a large hall. We were asked to sit down and have a cup of tea. Within half an hour four men walked in, and this was to be the first of many interrogations each of us had to go through. When they were finished with you, you were kept separate from the other fellows. They wanted to know everything; where you started, from where, how you got there and who was the leader who organized the escape and where he lived. The last question none of us wanted to answer and we told the interrogator that it would be too dangerous for that person to be known.

After a short time, they took us to their canteen, where a dinner was put on for the ten of us. Then they took us to another truck for transport to the railway station, with an escort of two policemen. Most of us were already asleep before the train pulled out. We were that tired.

On arrival in London, someone steered us into a room with twelve beds, army style. After an hour's rest, we each received two sets of clothing, all army issue. Then we were taken to the canteen and given soap, two towels, a toothbrush and paste, comb, shaving gear, fifty cigarettes and two Pounds Sterling for the rest of the week, which was two days. The money was for extra things like sweets and smokes. We were also given an information sheet with meal hours, doctor's visiting hours and so on. Things were really looking up now.

My school protected me

George Hansman

I finished my formal school years (seven years) plus two years of trade school in June, 1943. This became a dilemma for my parents, as I was now fifteen years old and many 16-year-olds were already being picked up by the Germans to do war work, such as building bunkers and other defense works.

Fortunately the school authorities recognized the problem and put me to work as a cleaner in my old school while I agreed to take some classes in drafting. During this same year I entered high school to obtain the necessary credentials to take an entrance exam to a higher technical college the following year. This program, which was very unusual, protected me during many raids by the Germans as my papers showed that I was a student and spent many hours in school.

Several times during the next years, the streets were blocked in our neighbourhood, which was a predominantly Jewish area. Jews, along with other able-bodied men, were picked up and transported to holding areas.

By the fall of 1944, college started its new year. Many sixteen, seventeen, and eighteen-year-olds entered school with dubious expectations since they were the age group the Germans were after for cheap labour. A few days after classes started, an urgent message came over the intercom that all classes were cancelled and that students were to return home without delay. Apparently the Resistance had tipped off the Dean that a raid on the college was in the making, and he therefore cancelled classes immediately. This was a brave thing to do, since the assistant Dean was a Nazi sympathizer and very much in favour of the German occupation.

At this time the Germans started to feel the pressure of their defeat in Normandy, and the Allied advances to the north and east. The Dutch railroad workers went on strike, paralyzing train movement throughout the Netherlands and especially to Germany. My Dad, a railroader, was on medical leave at the start of the strike, having burned his hand badly. He consequently was not really a striker. This actually gave him more freedom of movement as the others all had to be careful and sometimes go into hiding. This enabled him to be a messenger for the strikers and supply them with an income, as well as having contact with the Resistance through the Amsterdam police. Mysteriously, his hand never got better until the day the war ended.

During the winter of 1944-45 we listened to the radio in secret and received messages through the Resistance about how the Allied troops were advancing and digging in. We learned, of course, about the fiasco of them not being able to cross the rivers before the fall, which meant a catastrophe for western Holland where people were starving.

My friend and I spent a lot of time on the roof of our four-storey apartment building watching the Allied planes fly over on their way to Germany. Anti-aircraft guns were always in action but with few results, as the planes were flying at high altitudes. As spring came closer the anti-aircraft action decreased steadily, and our hopes climbed that it would soon be over. Fewer and fewer German troops were seen on the streets, and many reports told us that columns of soldiers had been seen going east towards Germany.

It was from the roof that we saw the first food drops by Allied planes a few days before the liberation of western Holland. These food drops saved many people from starvation, including myself, as I had not eaten during the previous three weeks.

Soon after, we heard rumors that the Allied troops had crossed the rivers and were advancing into northern Holland and Germany. Western Holland above the rivers was completely free of German troops by then, and the Resistance took over the policing along with the local police forces. Many people tried to settle scores with known Nazi sympathizers and collaborators, but for the most part the police kept things under control.

I was proud to do something for my country

Maria Pais

My father had a warehouse in IJmuiden. I don't remember exactly when, but at one point IJmuiden became an exclusion zone (*'Sperrgebiet'* in German), which meant that only the most essential people were allowed to stay there while everyone else had to leave. Any time you came into or went out of the area you had to show your identity card to prove that you lived there.

Of course the Germans came into Dad's business too, including the *Ortskommandant*, the German military commander in charge of a town or city. Any time this man placed an order it was I who had to deliver it to his office.

My father was in the Resistance, and I was enlisted for the cause as well. The secretary of the *Ortskommandant* was also in the Resistance, and any time I took an order there and had to wait in her office, she would give me papers, stamps, and so on. Since I was skinny as a rail and flat as a board at the age of fifteen, no one would notice a bit more bulk on my body. I was proud to do something for my country.

My father had hidden a radio in the warehouse. Every evening I listened to Radio England and took down the news in stenography, so that all the good news could be used in the illegal newsletter published by the Resistance.

Saved by
an unknown woman

Ben Meyer

msterdam, late 1943. I was eighteen and distributing extra ration cards to families who were hiding people. One day, at work, I was warned to go home because our network had been raided. My group gave me an address where I could go into hiding.

By the late fall of 1944 I had been in that house with several other men for many months, and seeing the beautiful sunshine I could not stand it any longer. I got the idea of taking my old bike and riding to the garden allotment of a friend on the Zuidelijke Wandelweg, a road through a park-like area at the southern edge of the city. There were quite a few people out enjoying the sunshine.

Then suddenly everyone started shouting and running around me. The Germans had closed off both entrances to the road and started to round up all the men. I was near the cemetery where my father was buried and was trying to get across it when I was caught. We were all put into a marching line and walked at gunpoint to the Apollo Hall, which was originally built for indoor tennis courts, but was now used as an assembly hall. The plan was to put the men onto barges to Germany. Not far from the hall, however, pandemonium broke out. A gunshot was fired and the guards all ran to the rear of the line.

Near the entrance of the Apollo hall, on each side of the road, stood many women watching what was going on. I did not think, just acted. I gave my bike to the man beside me, stepped out of the line, took the arm of the nearest woman and said, "Walk!"

We never spoke a word after that. We came to a canal called Ruysdaelkade, with a small ferry. I thanked the woman and hopped on the ferry. I don't remember how I got to Bosboom Toussaint Street, where I had been hiding, in another district of Amsterdam. I was in a daze.

What I do know is that, if it were not for that young woman, I would not now be telling this story, for later I heard that many men who were picked up during that raid had died of dysentery en route to the labour camps of Germany. Very few survived.

In his own bed

Michael Vanderboon

In the spring of 1944 it became clear that the occupiers of our land needed more slave labour for their factories in Germany, and for clearing debris after bombing raids. That's why they held razzias, raids, in all the occupied countries, including Holland. They would fence off some streets with barbed wire so no one could get in or out, and then search every house systematically for men aged seventeen to forty-five. Sometimes they would first notify the entire city that at a certain hour all the men had to stand by the curb with a blanket and some clothing. Then a big truck would pick them up and transport them to Germany.

Men found to be hiding would be punished, mistreated or sometimes shot. Towards the end of the war the soldiers sometimes shot through the walls or the floor just to scare people.

I lived with my father, mother, and sister in the Bezuidenhout, a section of The Hague. I was eight years old in 1943 and my sister barely three. My father, just like many other men, was hiding in our house, under the living room floor. The crawl space there measured fifteen by twenty feet and had a sand floor. It was only three feet high so you could never stand up and stretch.

In the living room we had a coal stove against one of the walls but it was never used because we had no coal to burn. On the mantel stood a clock and some photos. When you moved the stove aside there was a hatch in the floor, under which my father was hidden. He had a mattress, blankets, pillow, flashlight, and a small radio, something that was strictly forbidden. If you were found with one of those you'd be sent to prison or a concentration camp. My father therefore listened only when there was a BBC program from England. Sometimes I lay with my ear to the floor, trying to listen. Not that I could understand it, but I always heard the first four notes of Beethoven's Fifth Symphony, their signal. It was dangerous to listen to the radio because sometimes there were trucks patrolling the streets with equipment to detect the signals. The flashlight was a dynamo, hand-powered. As long as you kept pumping it you had light.

My father had been hiding for six months under that floor already, and only came out once a week to sleep in his own bed. At mealtime, or what passed for meals since there was very little to eat, Mom and I would push the stove aside. We also gave him other stuff he needed like soap and water and a toothbrush. We had to be careful so nobody could tell there was a fourth person in the house, like having four plates or cups on the table. You couldn't be careful enough, and we children were warned every day to say nothing about our father. It was our secret.

It so happened that Dad decided to sleep in his own bed for a change. After all, things had been peaceful lately in terms of raids. Everything went well until five in the morning when it was just getting light. Suddenly the doorbell rang.

My father, still dazed with sleep, for some reason stepped out of bed and walked to the front door. The door had a little window in it with a flimsy curtain in front of it, so that you could see out but they couldn't see in. My father looked out and almost died of fright. There stood two German soldiers and an officer. I'd never seen Dad jump into his hole so quickly! We had to push the stove back into place too, of course. By that time the soldiers were just banging on the door.

My mother rushed to open the door while trying to control her nerves, and I was trying to calm my little sister Ronnie. We were really scared.

The soldiers stepped into the hall and asked Mom where her husband was. She told them he was working in Germany, for the Wehrmacht. Luckily her German was pretty good, which calmed them down a bit, but even so they searched the house from top to bottom. With Dad so nearby we held our breath.

At last, after what seemed an eternity, they were finished. They had found nothing, but the most dangerous moment was still to come.

Just as they were ready to leave, the officer bent down, and kneeling by my little sister he started talking to her. He knew a bit of broken Dutch, and had apparently learned that you can trick little kids into telling some surprising truths.

"Where's Daddy, sweetheart?" he asked her. I thought Mom was going to have a heart attack.

"There's my Daddy", said Ronnie, pointing at the stove. For a moment my mother was dumbstruck, but then she quickly walked to the mantel and took down Dad's photo.

"Yes, that's Daddy", she told Ronnie. Her quick reaction saved my father's life.

The officer smiled at my little sister and walked out behind his soldiers. We waited a few minutes before opening the hatch for Dad. Crying, and still nervous wrecks, we fell into each other's arms. Little Ronnie, not understanding the fuss maybe, cried right along with us.

Six months later my father was picked up anyway, when he and a neighbour were sawing down a tree for fuel in the middle of the night. Both of them were sent to a camp in Germany.

How my brother escaped

Corry Spruit-Degeling

My brother Jaap was living and working in Haarlem with his wife Jo, who was two weeks away from having their first child. They had purchased a very large old baby buggy. Their friends and neighbours laughed and teased him about the size of the buggy. Since Jaap was a small man, they said he could fit into the buggy and his wife could push him around. He then climbed into the buggy, which brought more laughter.

As Jaap was making deliveries for the butcher shop where he worked, he found himself in the wrong place at the wrong time. He was captured in a German razzia and was brought to the Ripperda barracks in the north of Haarlem.

His wife received a letter that Jaap was going to be transported to Germany the next day and she would be allowed to say goodbye. Jo, of course, was beside herself. The butcher's wife, Mrs. Eskers, was a close friend. She reminded Jo how Jaap had fit into the baby buggy and that they should try to rescue him. Mrs. Eskens decided to undertake the extremely dangerous escapade since she did not want to endanger the life of the unborn child.

As she wheeled the buggy into the barracks square where the prisoners were assembled, she asked the men to gather round the buggy and pretend to admire the imaginary baby. Jaap jumped into the buggy with his knees up to his chin. He was covered with blankets and a woollen buggy cover. Mrs. Eskens then walked away with the buggy. Looking back at the group, she was crying and waving goodbye with a large kerchief. It was an Oscar-worthy performance for sure. She then quickly took Jaap to our aunt's house where he hid until nightfall. He left during the night dressed as a woman and stayed in hiding until the war ended.

Their baby was born a few weeks later, and I often had to go through many checkpoints to bring Jaap's wife and child any extra food our family could find.

There were many ordinary, everyday people like Mrs. Eskens who became heroes during the war. These brave, strong people deserve to be remembered for their part in winning the small battles.

An 11-year-old courier

Tom de Vries

In 1944 the food situation in Amsterdam became precarious, and for us five children in a high school teacher's family, hunger was our daily diet. The situation became so bad that our church organized the removal of the most malnourished children to Andijk and Hoorn, where church families were ready to take them. My parents decided that my younger brother and I would have to leave Amsterdam too.

One day after school we were taken to the Amsterdam harbour where we boarded a small inland freighter. There were ten or fifteen of us, children and adults, some also from Rotterdam. Above deck there was cargo destined for Enkhuizen. The trip was made in complete darkness and silence to evade German detection. In Enkhuizen we were met by the host families. I was taken on the back of a bike. My brother was taken to Hoorn and I did not see him or hear from him until after Liberation. I was taken to Andijk to a family with ten children, the Kistemakers. They must have figured one more mouth to feed would be easy. However, I had contracted scabies on the ship, which is contagious, so the Andijk people moved me to a childless couple. Unbeknownst to me, these people were heavily involved in the Resistance movement.

Mr. Nanne Vriend went daily to check on his flower bulb sheds, spread throughout the polder there. One day he invited me along on his flat bottom boat, with a long pole to push the boat along and steer it. Inside some of the flower bulb sheds were young men hiding from the occupiers, and I met them all and became friends with them. They lived behind rows of bulb boxes. They had put up strings for drying tobacco leaves. They used thin paper from a pocket Bible to roll their cigarettes.

Being eleven years old and wanting to be grown up and accepted, I also started to smoke. Since I could handle the small boat by myself with the long pole, I was asked if I would go to these bulb sheds every few days to bring supplies to the men, and also messages. I was used as a courier, of course, because I was unafraid, a real Amsterdam youngster.

During this whole period - about a year - I had no communication with my parents. No phone, no mail. I counted it a blessing to be used as an eleven-year-old courier!

Did they know
their little boy was safe?

Henry Niezen

I was one of about 350,000 men who were on the run and hiding from the Germans in 1943. This story is about what happened in Driebergen, a small town in the province of Utrecht.

What do people do when facing suppression and adversity? They find solace in each other. They go to the church of their particular faith to listen to the good news and sing hymns together.

But who is sitting in the pew close to you? It could be someone who took advantage of scarcity and is profiting from the black market. Or someone who would report to the enemy anyone heard speaking against the 'New Order' of the NSB and the Nazis. There is danger both in the church and outside of it.

On one particular Sunday in 1943 the members of the church who were assigned to watch at the door saw German soldiers outside, lying in wait for young men to come out, to take them away to work in the *'Arbeitseinsatz'*. The young men were an easy target.

But the soldiers were spotted. A secret sign was given, perhaps a cough into a handkerchief. It was enough, and the minister knew there was a razzia going on.

The minister completed his sermon; the last hymn was announced, and all the men of the targeted age knew that giving this particular hymn was a sign of danger. All these men would, after the service, go silently through the back door to the stairs into the church tower. Halfway up there was a secret panel hiding a room. The men were safe there. Only the minister and the custodian, who lived next door, knew where to direct them. Even their wives and the maid, a clever young woman, were unable to find the place when challenged.

After the coast was clear, the young men could go home, but no more than two at a time.

At the same church, the minister's boys were playing outside with a three-year-old Jewish boy. German soldiers arrested the little boy's father and mother for shipment to Westerbork and from there to Auschwitz or Sobibor. What were their thoughts when they were arrested? Did they know their little boy was safe?

The custodian and his wife took the little boy in and raised him as their own. He never saw his own parents again.

So terribly mean

Nel Meyer

I was thirteen years old in June, 1943, when I wrote in my diary about the Nazi soldiers who came looking for a little Jewish boy we had kept hidden. 'I find it so terribly mean, that there were five of them to take away a little two-year-old child', I wrote. 'I find it so pitiable.'

This is what happened: My sister, Gerda, had come home in November, 1942 from the day care where she worked, and told my parents that one of the children had not been called for by his parents. My parents asked her to go back and bring the little boy to us. Neighbours were told he was a nephew from England who had tuberculosis, a cover story to explain why Paul was circumcised. All went well until the following June. Mother and I had been shopping and when we came home, Gerda and little Paul were gone. We looked around and asked the neighbour if they knew where they had gone. She told us the Gestapo had been there and left again. Also that the Gestapo had been at the house earlier when nobody was home. When Mother asked her why they had not warned us, she said, "You didn't tell us Paul was a Jew, so we didn't think we had to tell you."

We went to Aunt Annie, my mother's best friend, and there they were. Gerda had told the Gestapo our cover story. They did not take Paul then, but had said they would be back at seven that evening.

This was discussed at length, and it was decided that

the best course of action was to obey Nazi orders. My mother, Annie, and Paul were all at our house at 7 p.m. when they came: three Gestapo men and two Dutch Nazis. Paul had to go with them. My mother asked if she could carry him down to the car, and did. While the men put Paul in the car Mom asked the driver quietly where he would be taken, and at great risk to himself he whispered, "To the day care".

Mom was heartbroken. The next day she went to see the manager of the day care, a Jewish lady. The Germans liked to put Jews in charge of Jews. After some hesitation, since she did not know if she could trust this woman, Mom explained what had happened and that she wanted Paul back. The woman agreed to help. She would put Paul in a closet on the second floor the next day, when the children were to be transported to wherever it was they were going.

The following day Mom went to the day care. After the trucks with children and adults had left, she took the route given to her the previous day. She had to go through the house next door, through the garden, and climb a fence. She went into the empty day care and found Paul, dressed as a little girl, quietly waiting in the closet. She did not dare run but walked as quickly as possible to the Central Station where she boarded a train to Breda, where my father had gone.

At the second stop a couple of Gestapo men entered the car and sat down across from her. Her heart almost stopped when she recognized one of them as one of the five who had taken Paul away. She kept Paul's attention on what was outside the train windows, and got out at the next station. Then she took the next train, and kept changing trains randomly until, after crisscrossing the country, she arrived in Breda.

She left Paul with my Dad, who was staying with his brother's family, and went back to Amsterdam. There she contacted the Resistance group to which she belonged (Group 2000; her code name was 'Aunt Willemien'). They gave her the address of a family in Stadskanaal, where she eventually took Paul. He stayed there until after the war.

Because of Mom's success in hiding Paul, she was from time to time given the names of children and the addresses of people who would take them. She rescued thirty-one children this way, only one of their mothers survived. Many years later this mother invited Mom to the child's Bar Mitzvah, a great honour.

Mom was active in the Resistance until the end of the war. When she ran out of time to deliver ration cards to people in hiding, she sent me on those errands. They won't suspect a young girl, were her thoughts. Also she gave me photographs of the Dutch royal family in Canada to give to the principal of my school, who would sell them to other teachers and parents. This was a way to raise money to help people survive.

One day I left my school bag with schoolbooks in the tram. When I told Mom about it she sent me to the head office to get it back. My friend and I went there and I asked if they had found my school bag. I had to describe the contents, which I did. With a wink the man said, "And something else, eh?" because between the pages of the atlas and the German Literature books were photos of the royal family. I was shaking, and felt very lucky that I had encountered a 'good' guy. One never knew; there were so many traitors.

Because of Mom's Resistance work we had to go into hiding several times. I missed a lot of school. One time Mom had forgotten her mother's gold jewellery, which was needed to trade for food eventually. I went back home to fetch it, which was a scary journey even though I was an 'innocent child'. I had to watch carefully to make sure I was not followed.

Paul's parents had been arrested and tortured before being sent to a concentration camp. They had met my parents only once, but my father had been wearing his postal uniform, with #2 on the collar. In the end the mother told her torturers that. When the Gestapo contacted the post office to find out who #2 was, a department head who was a collaborator answered the phone, and did not warn Dad. However, the Gestapo never followed up because they were moving from Euterpe Street to the Roelof Hart Square, and we had moved also. Somehow they forgot about us. How lucky we were.

In February of 1945 I was one of the lucky twenty or so girls who, through the church synod, were smuggled by barge out of Amsterdam to Wormerveer in the province of North Holland. We stayed at the clubhouse of the Verkade chocolate factories. We were well fed and kept busy with chores, study and entertainment. Arriving home after the Liberation I felt ashamed of being so healthy while my family was so frail.

Arrest in the night

Atty Prosper

We lived in Drachten, Friesland. We were hiding Jews in our house: Jan and Marie van Santen and their daughter Sonia. Two resistance workers, Mient Veenstra and Sietze van de Boom, had arranged for this as they knew that the Van Santens needed a place to stay. We also had another man hiding with us, Bob Bolt, who was eighteen.

On March 25, 1944, the SS came in the night. They picked up Jan, Marie and Sonia, as well as my mother and brother, and took them to Drachten first, then by tram to Leeuwarden. My mother was wearing wooden shoes. I wanted to give her shoes and a Bible but I was chased away. Like criminals, surrounded by soldiers, they were taken first to Grundmann (*SS-Oberscharfuhrer Friedrich Grundmann, Kriminal-Assistent with Sipo and the S.D. in Leeuwarden*), then to jail. Jan and Marie and Sonia were sent to Germany within days. My mother talked to them still and told them, "Believe in the Lord Jesus Christ and you will be saved." My brother was sent to the concentration camp at Vught, and later to Camp Rheine in Germany. He experienced a lot of hardship but after the war he came home on foot in August of 1945, because there was nothing yet, no transportation. He was in bad shape, mentally and physically.

So there I was on the farm, all alone. The neighbours helped and we had a hired man who knew the work, but my mother was in jail. There was still a tram going to Leeuwarden then, so I went there to talk to Grundmann, and got permission to visit my mother. Grundmann's office was in the Burger Weeshuis (Civic Orphanage), and later, when the Canadians liberated us, they found all kinds of torture instruments in the cellar. I told Grundmann that my mother had to come home because the farm needed her. "No," he said, "she's going to Vught because she was hiding Jews". "No," I said, "not Jews, just evacuees". "No, Jews," he said.

My mother told him the same thing as I had said. So I went to Leeuwarden twice a week, always to see him, and to the jail. After six weeks my mother came home. She had to pay 300 marks. So we accomplished that, but there was no pleasure in it. We didn't know where my brother was. Our friends, the Jews, were gone. Bob Bolt was gone. Sonia and I were the same age and we had always had a lot of fun together.

In August my oldest brother came home. He was married and had kids. Then, during the night, he was taken from his bed, and with nine other men, was taken to the Leeuwarden jail. Ten men in one cell, and it was a hot August. So then it was back to Leeuwarden for me, together with my brother's wife. We asked for Grundmann and first they said that he was not there, but we stayed and after a while they called us in. Grundmann recognized me because I always wore the same blouse, and I told him: "my other brother is in Germany and we need this brother on the farm, and you told me before that if he got picked up, to come and see you". That wasn't exactly true, but I had a small bottle of gin with me and set that on the floor beside me. He then told me that my brother was free to go and that I could take him home. He was free. So we went home on the tram again but we were going crazy with itch from the fleas. I don't know what happened to the other nine men.

That *Landwacht* was something else. They were a paramilitary group organized by the Germans, but consisting of Dutch collaborators. They took everything. Maybe the Germans too, but... we had hidden a pig and they found that. Gold rings, crocheted bedspreads, spoons and forks, a milk can full of oil, cabbage seed, and lots more. Later on a member of the *Landwacht* came by with his gun across his back, wearing my brother's pants.

The closet ceiling was lower

Cornelis Langewis

When Holland was occupied by Germany, all the news we got was German controlled and laced with German propaganda. To receive dependable world and war news, I listened to the BBC. But not for long; Germans ordered that all radios should be turned in. Nobody was supposed to have a radio.

I looked around and found a radio that had been put together by an amateur in the 1920s, and looked like it too. But when plugged in, some sound came out. The owner wanted a lot of money for it, but I bought it anyway and turned it in, thus getting my certificate showing that I had turned in a radio. It was a good paper to have as later our house was searched twice.

I had noticed that the ceiling of a closet in the living room was about a foot and a half lower than the ceiling of the living room itself. Also, the space between the living room ceiling and the floor of the upstairs bedroom was more than a foot. I already knew that last bit, because I had hidden an expensive bike there. Therefore the space between the closet ceiling and the upstairs floor was more than two and a half feet, enough space to hide our radio. In it went, tuned (softly) to the BBC and connected to something that did not look like a switch, but was.

At seven in the evening I would turn the radio on, stand on a chair, stick my head into the closet, and listen to dependable news, which I then spread around. So far, so good. But then D-Day came and Allied forces marched through France and Belgium and liberated the southern part of Holland, the part south of the wide rivers that divide The Netherlands in two. They left the northern part occupied by Germany and turned east, apparently hoping to get to Berlin before the Russians got there.

Conditions in the German-occupied part of Holland were terrible, cut off from major food supplies and fuel. The coal mines were in the southern, liberated part, and out of reach for us north of the rivers. This period, known as the Hunger Winter, was very bad. Towards the end of the war American bombers parachuted food packages to us. Sweden, through the Red Cross, sent tons of flour.

Electricity was cut off as the main power plants were running out of fuel. In the street where we lived, there was a large pastry shop and bakery, and they had to bake bread from the Swedish flour. For that, electricity was needed. The bakery was connected to an underground cable, which was powered up again by the power company. The houses on our street were also connected to this cable, but had been disconnected by the power company. Our house and those of three of our neighbours were hooked up to a small fuse box mounted on a brick wall. It contained four main fuses which were removed by the power company when they restored power to the underground cable that enabled the bakery to bake bread. To open the fuse box, a small tool was needed. I had such a tool and as I did not want to lose contact with the BBC and its dependable news, I decided to hook up to the power source. I told my next-door neighbour that I could hook him up so he would have power too, but only for small lights. "No electric heating or cooking or anything that makes noise, and be sure that no lights can be seen from the outside."

He was delighted. He was a professional photographer and could do some darkroom work. The second neighbour liked it too, but his wife got into a frenzy. "No, no, leave us out. If they catch us we might end up in a concentration camp!" The third neighbour was very happy to get hooked up, so in the evening I opened the fuse box and put three main fuses in. Everything seemed all right at first, but then I got a warning. "Cor, they suspect that electricity is being used illegally and they might come around to read the meters to find the culprit." So I warned my neighbours and left it up to them if they wanted to keep using power. I didn't want to give up my news source or electric lights.

Since the kWh meters in Holland were inside the house, I could work unnoticed. I broke the seal on the meter, opened the meter case, took out the counter and turned it back by hand to what I thought was the reading shown on the last power bill. I put it back together the way it had been, and added a by-pass around the meter so power used was no longer registered. It all worked out fine.

I never told my parents

John van der Meer

One day I was approached by an older boy, about sixteen years of age, who asked me to join the Resistance movement. I was interested but when he wanted to teach me how to shoot a gun I got cold feet. It was a good thing I refused. Within a few weeks the Gestapo rolled up the group and according to his neighbours the boy was shot while trying to run away. If he had not died right there, who knows; he might have given me away. I never told my parents about this, of course.

Around the same time we heard that a store nearby, where only Germans could shop, had been overrun by a crowd because it was rumoured that the store had cooking oil in stock. We used cooking oil to burn an oil lamp at night. I went over but the show had finished when I got there. In the meantime a patrol car with Germans had already arrived there and had arrested eight people at random, whom they lined up in front of the store and shot. No one was allowed to remove the bodies, which were left outside the store as an example.

Not long thereafter a cart full of potatoes, which I had been following, parked in front of a German office. People crowded around it and I joined them. The two men in charge of the cart started to throw the potatoes out and I got a good portion of them stuck under my shirt and made a getaway. The crowd had been very threatening to the two men. On my way home I saw a German patrol car driving fast towards where the cart was, and once again I got away in time.

With two other boys I went to the park to cut a tree down for firewood. We were cutting it into pieces when a German patrol car got to us. They were friendly and told us to carry on. After some hours we had the job done, and when the Germans came back and ordered us to load up a truck we got the picture. They gave us a kick in the behind and fired a gun over our heads. I wet my pants; yes, sure I did! We ran away, hearing them laugh. I ran so fast I set a world record, I swear.

Aunt Dinie's memories

Henk van der Meulen

In the summer of 2010 I visited my aunt Dinie in Huntsville, Ontario, just before her 83rd birthday. I mentioned the wood veneer inlay her husband had made while in hiding during the war. She could not recall it specifically but it led us to talking of certain incidents about that time.

Henk, her future husband then, had been in hiding from the Germans like several others from Zwartsluis. He was staying in Aalten with the Te Hennepe family who operated a carpentry shop. The year was probably 1943. Henk and Dinie had been seeing each other for a while and one evening Dinie's father, who was involved in the Resistance, told Henk that his name appeared on a German hit list. Henk planned to contact the leader of the Aalten Resistance, a man named Wikkerink, the following day to find another hiding place. However, he left it too late.

That night he woke up to find himself surrounded by five or six SS men with weapons drawn. He was taken to the nearby town of Winterswijk and imprisoned for later transport to Germany. Around that time, the Germans burned the Wikkerink house to the ground. Rijk, the youngest brother, had been hiding in Aalten as well, with Ter Haar, the local miller. He was captured also and sent to work in the industrial Ruhr district of Germany, from which he later escaped.

Somehow word got back to Zwartsluis that Henk was being held in custody. Reinder, Henk's oldest brother, decided to go immediately to see what could be done to prevent Henk from being sent to Germany. His only available means of transport was a bicycle. The distance from Zwartsluis to Aalten is sixty miles as the crow flies. On winding, poorly maintained rural roads the distance was likely 80 miles or more. It would have taken him twelve to fifteen hours to make the trip under these adverse conditions.

Reinder went to Aalten first, and it was decided that he and Dinie would go to Winterswijk and try to gain Henk's release. It must be remembered that Reinder ran considerable risk of being arrested, or worse. Had the Germans known that Reinder was the local commander of the Resistance, he would have been put against a wall and shot, according to Dinie. He probably travelled with forged identity papers.

Appearing before the German authorities, Reinder and Dinie had to show their 'ausweis', the hated identity cards, which showed the birth dates also. Looking at Dinie, the commandant, who appeared to be a not-unsympathetic collaborator, asked, "Do your parents know that you are seeing a much older man?" Dinie was sixteen at the time, with Henk eight years older.

The result of their appeal was that Henk was transferred to Zwolle, about ten miles from Zwartsluis. He was put to work for the Germans there but fled at the first opportunity and went into hiding again. It was many months before he and Dinie saw each other again.

A carbide lamp

Karel Stuut

In our home in Haarlem, my father made a fake floor in one of the living room cupboards. This fake floor could be raised on hinges and gave access to a crawl space under the floors of the living room and dining room. When there was a raid by German officers in our street, looking for men to go to work camps in Germany, they searched every home on our street except those of the NSB-members who were on their side. During these raids, when my father was home, he went through the fake floor and hid from the Germans. When they searched the living room my father hid under the dining room floor, and when they were searching the dining room he crawled under the living room floor. He knew that officers sometimes shot several bullets through the floor during these raids.

On our street, Pieter Kies Street, there was a milk processing plant where milk was processed for the Germans. Because of this plant there was always electricity on our street. My father bypassed the electrical meter circuit and so was able to use his electric drill on our manual coffee grinder in the kitchen to grind wheat into flour so my mother could bake bread and make pancakes.

I remember that because we were not allowed to use electricity, our living room was illuminated by a carbide lamp. There were rocks of carbide.

We had nothing to burn in our fireplace to heat the living room, and so my father built two small wood burners out of heavy steel sheeting. Each one was about twelve inches high and eight inches in diameter. There was a grill at about one inch from the bottom, upon which a stack of small branches and wood cuttings were piled and set on fire. It provided some heat but also smoke in our living room. My mother always had a kettle of water on these wood burners so she could make tea.

Sometimes our home was raided by the Germans to collect copper and brass items. They needed these materials for the manufacture of ammunition. We had several things hidden behind a secret wall panel in a bedroom closet. A couple of them did not fit in this narrow space, so Dad buried these in the backyard during the night. After the war we were unable to find them, because my father had forgotten where he had buried them. I am sure they're still there today.

He escaped all the raids

Yvonne Harvey Shea

My mother couldn't stand the cold, so Dad and a friend went to the woods to get firewood. That friend worked for the Germans in the school behind our house. Dad had a small wagon, and the two of them took that along to transport the wood. While they were chopping away, the Germans did nothing, because officially the wood was intended for the school so that the soldiers there would be warm. On the way back, however, one-third of the load went into our house for fuel.

Another time, my brother, stepbrother and I went to the place where trains arrived, loaded with coal for the Germans. We had little bags and picked up as much as possible of the coal bits that had fallen on the ground. Even if that would only keep us warm for a couple of hours it didn't matter. Towards evening all three of us looked a mess, so we headed home. Two soldiers came along and they had to see what was in the bags. When they saw the bits of coal they made us dump it all. So we had nothing to show for all the work.

My father escaped all the razzias, the raids. We had a house guest, Uncle Henk, who was too old to be taken away to the work camps, so it was usually he who answered the door when the soldiers came knocking. Sometimes Dad answered the door, but only after smearing a thick layer of ointment on his face to make it look as though he had scabies. The soldiers wanted nothing to do with that, so away they went.

We were told
to keep our mouth shut

Bouk Jobsis

There was no electricity, although if you put a knitting needle in the meter you could tap into the German power supply.

When there were razzias you had to remove the needle, put the seal back on the meter, and hide your father in his hiding place between the first and second storey of the house. Then you put the linoleum, the rug, and a piece of furniture on top of the opening. Then mother would open the door. We kids were told to keep our mouths shut. It was safer that way.

We lived with fear. Besides the house searches there were sirens going off when bombing by Allied forces was imminent. They targeted the airport but often missed. Decades later, sirens still frightened me.

My father had his year of birth on his identity card put back a few years, trying to avoid being sent to Germany to work. Still, when the need for labour became great, the Germans might send any man to work in their factories. We knew that starvation and possibly death waited there.

I saw them
being loaded into a truck

Susan Rombeek

Our house in The Hague was in Frambozenstraat (Raspberry Street), at the corner of Meloenstraat (Melon Street). Corner houses were chosen by the Germans to distribute their flyers and orders (Befehls) to the rest of the people in the street. Many times we were awakened early in the morning by German soldiers who would kick our door and demand that we distribute their befehls. I remember that they would come in, looking for copper or blankets, and they even took a winter coat from my father.

Then came the razzias for bicycles, and young men. Our neighbour on Meloenstraat had five boys. Four were old enough to be sent to Germany. Our house had windows facing Meloenstraat and their front door on Frambozenstraat. We realized that the Germans were confused about this, so when the soldiers were coming into the neighbours' house we told the boys to jump over our fence and hide under our floor until they were gone. It was very frightening. Unfortunately, even though my father begged them to stay a little longer, the boys felt it was better to jump back across the fence because the soldiers had left their house and were now coming to ours. However, one German was still standing in their garden when they jumped over the fence. They were caught, and I saw them being loaded into a truck for shipment to Germany. It was so sad.

My uncle told us he had spent a whole day in an empty YMCA building, crouched in the little cabinet under a sink, before he could find a safe house. Germans had been sitting on the counter above him, he said.

We also had a bike razzia. Everyone was warned not to go into certain streets, as soldiers would take your bike. We kids ran around warning everyone. When my grandfather was stopped, he immediately started limping and acting senile, and they let him keep his bike.

Then the Germans started firing V1 and V2 rockets from Ockenburg airfield to England. Every time one was launched we stood still and listened, because sometimes they would come down soon after they were launched. One day I was standing in front of our window upstairs and saw a huge fireball coming over the roofs. It exploded and the bomb landed in Indigostraat (Indigo Street), killing many people.

My father was involved with an illegal paper, and my brother Niek and I were often asked to distribute these. We did this mostly close to dark, as there was a curfew and we figured they would not be too strict with kids.

One day Dad came home very upset. His friend had been caught and was shot on the Waalsdorper Vlakte (Plains of Waalsdorp), where many Resistance fighters were executed.

They had to walk 30 miles

Anne Hendren

During the war my family lived in Utrecht, where my father was a doctor. As the war went on, the German occupation began to change our lives. Rationing of food products had already started during the summer of 1940. Every Sunday morning Dad would rush downstairs to grab the newspaper, De Telegraaf. Every Sunday a new group of merchandise, food, or textiles was added to the ration cards. Protein products such as meat, butter and milk were targeted first, for the simple reason that those products were all being shipped to Germany. Slowly but surely Holland was being strangled as its food supply was looted.

By the end of 1943 our country had been stripped of all its valuable works of art, with the paintings and sculptures given to high ranking German officials. Men were rounded up and shipped to Germany to work in munitions factories and to dig trenches. These razzias were unannounced. Blocks and homes would be cordoned off, the houses searched, bicycles taken, and the men hauled away at gunpoint. Many of the men went under cover and tried to stay hidden for the duration of the war. Hiding places consisted of closets, hay lofts, garden sheds, and cellars, among others. When proclamations were made ordering men to come forward and enlist, very few came. That meant the razzias continued.

Late one afternoon a huge column of men came past our house. They had been forced to walk the thirty miles from The Hague and Rotterdam, and were ready to drop from fatigue. Anyone who did was shot by the German guards. Suddenly there was gunfire, and in the resulting confusion many of the men fled into the houses along our street. Our friends and neighbours, the Schmidt family, were able to quickly hide several of those men. These were the lucky ones, the rest shuffled on at gunpoint.

It was difficult for Dutch people to get credible news about the war. What was on the radio and in the newspapers was German propaganda. Listening clandestinely to short wave radio and the BBC to find out what was really happening kept up the spirits of the people. But if caught doing so, you got a severe penalty.

Neighbours of ours in Utrecht, a Roman Catholic family with nine children and the owners of a couple of shoe stores, had a son who was a priest. He had access to a radio, and thus to BBC news. He shared that news with a number of people by coming to the side entrance of our corner house and quickly handing over a tiny piece of paper with the main news typed on it, and then quickly taking off again. Perhaps other people seeing this man in his black cassock coming to our house so often thought that we were converting to Catholicism! The snippets of news he provided were very important. The worse the war went for the Germans, the more propaganda they sent out. We already thought of it as mostly hogwash, but being able to hear the truth gave us hope and a positive perspective.

One evening after dark we heard many loud German voices, and someone banged on our front door. There was another razzia in our part of town, and any men they found were taken prisoner. Mom opened our front door to find two young SS soldiers, maybe eighteen years old, holding guns. They wanted *Herr Doktor* who was upstairs in the surgery. As Pap heard them coming up the stairs he quickly put on his white coat and asked them if they had a toothache. They said *Nein*, but *Herr Doktor* had to come along immediately.

At gunpoint Pap changed into an overcoat, said goodbye to all of us, and went with them. To find out where he was being taken, my sister Hennie and I followed them to the center of town and saw hundreds of men in the town square. That was all we could tell Mom when we returned home.

Just before the 8 p.m. curfew, Pap came through the front door! We could not believe our eyes. It turned out that he had forged documents, complete with stamps and signatures, which said he was the head of a surgical unit and that he was indispensable. He and a colleague who also had forged papers persuaded the German officials to release them. For security reasons Dad had never told anyone about these papers. But they worked, and thankfully he never had to use them again.

The men who had been rounded up that night were all herded onto freight trains which took them to Germany to work in the ammunition factories.

My Dad told me to sing

Catherina de Leeuw

We too had house searching. My Dad told me to sit on this chair and sing. The chair was placed over a place where you could go underground. No basement, just a hole in the ground. Dad had illegal papers down there.

So I sang. The Germans came in and one said he had a girl at home who was my age. So they did not search our house. The Lord protected us all through the war.

I saw their drawn bayonets

Schelte (Sam) Brandsma

Visiting *Omke* (Uncle) Jitze and *Muoike* (Aunt) Hiltje was always great fun. Their bake shop in Hantumhuizen, in the heart of Friesland, had great attraction for us. We were always much fussed over and spoiled with cookies and stuff. The gooseberries and red currants also tasted great. Their two daughters helped in the bake shop and went out to peddle the bread and other baked goods door to door.

It was now 1944, and wartime had greatly restricted normal life on our small mixed farm in the centre of Lioessens, which was a small community in the north of Friesland. We had been angry when we lost our horse, beautiful "Bruntje", to the Germans. Now a summons had been posted that all males between 18 and 25 must report to work for the failing German war machine. Like most young men, I ignored the summons and kept on milking cows and working in the fields.

We'd had someone hiding with us for six months, for whom we had made a hiding place upstairs. Someone had betrayed him, and he had to leave. He was later arrested, never to return. Now the two-by two pie-shaped corner beside the upstairs bedroom was to be mine, if it was ever needed. We had made plans what to do in case of a razzia. We were nervous and fearful, never knowing when one might take place.

We were all sound asleep around midnight one day in early September of 1944. Only my oldest sister Japke and her boyfriend, Ep, from Sneek, who had come courting, were still up. Ep was 25 but had forged papers stating that he was 28.

A loud banging woke us all to the grim reality of German soldiers at the front door. Dad was already there, asking loudly what they wanted. I slipped out of bed and quickly backed into my triangular hiding spot, then tapped on the floor three times to indicate to Dad that I was hidden. Dad let the two soldiers in and kept telling them there was nobody there.

The soldiers started searching the house. The ladder in the hall had been pulled up to avoid quick access. But the Germans went around the back and climbed the ladder to the hay loft. I could see them coming toward the bedroom with their bayonets drawn, shining flashlights around. I was shaking uncontrollably and feared I was going to rattle the plywood and give myself away. Japke had crawled into my bed so they would not find a warm bed with nobody in it. Ep had tucked himself in the other bed with his dress shirt still on.

I prayed, "Oh Lord, please!"

The soldiers pulled Ep out of bed and demanded papers. These satisfied them and they pursued him no farther. I lay stretched out with my hand on a piece of plywood. Some sacks of grain provided a bit of barrier between the stamping boots and my pounding heart.

At last they retreated through the hay, poking their bayonets in, trying to find any person who might be hiding. Thank God - they were leaving! Could it be true that I had been spared?

After a while we all gathered, all shaken up, wondering if they would return.

Omke Jitze and *Muoike* Hiltje had already offered that I could come down there when things got too hot at home. We all agreed that this was hot enough. Packing a few clothes and saying our goodbyes was done hastily. It was two in the morning and pitch dark outside when I rode off to Hantumhuizen. It was after curfew, so every sound scared me during my forty-five minute bike ride.

How good it was to enter the bake shop once again, with its fragrance and welcome. Grateful for my escape, they quickly made another hiding spot. I stayed out of sight for the remaining months of the war. I helped in the bake shop, always careful not to be seen. I missed the outdoors, Dad and Mom, my brothers and sisters, my friends and the village.

Finally the great news was shouted from house to house, *"Wy binne fry!"* - we are free. A feeling that cannot be described rushed through my whole being. There was life, real life, just ahead of us. Oane, who had been hiding next door, came out too and together we jumped on our bikes to go to Dokkum and see the Canadian soldiers who had liberated us. I saw the spring landscape as never before. Chills ran up and down my spine. Freedom! Freedom!

A nine-day novena

Doortje Shover

My parents lived on Boezem Singel, a canal in the center of Rotterdam, across from a cattle market. They had chosen this location for the wonderful and colourful view of the market. On Tuesdays the farmers would come down and sell their horses, cows, sheep, and goats. The sale was always done by handshake, never a contract. Horses were led around an island in the middle of the market; then their teeth were checked, which led to a sale, or not.

My father owned a small business about a ten minute walk from our house. It had been completely bombed at the start of the war. Much of our neighbourhood lay in ashes but our block of houses luckily was spared. My father had invested in silver coins, and all his money had melted in the tremendous fire after the bombing. He lost everything. Determined to continue working he set up a new business in the attic, the third floor. I was born on June 30, 1941.

In November, 1944, the Germans came to Boezem Singel where we lived, rang the doorbell of every house, and told the inhabitants that all men had to come to the cattle market across from us. They said they would examine every house and if they found a man in the house, the house would be burned down with everyone in it. They were planning a Razzia, rounding up men to work in Germany.

All the men were taken away, and the first night they slept in the Heineken brewery not too far from our house. The next day there were taken to a church in Putten, in the province of Gelderland.

On the night my father was taken away, my mother, desperate, went to our church to talk to the priest. He warned her that she was not supposed to be outside as there was an 8 p.m. curfew in place, imposed by the Germans. My mother said she wanted to start a novena, which is a nine-day prayer, and that she was hoping my father would be back on the ninth day. She was, in fact, convinced that my father would do so.

Meanwhile, my father had arrived in Putten with all the men from our neighbourhood. Outside the church was a urinal for men, and my father noticed that men went to use it and that some did not come back. He decided to give it a try. By the door stood either a friendly German or a Dutch military policeman (*marechaussee*). He allowed my father to use the urinal, and as my father left it, two women came by, took him by the arm, and led him away. They sheltered him, fed him, told him about the dangers, and prepared him for the long walk home to Rotterdam. They told him to walk during the night and try to find shelter on farms during the day. They told him which farms had inhabitants that collaborated with the Germans. Several times my father was warned by other walkers about a danger spot ahead, and to change his direction.

On the ninth day my mother heard a sound by the door downstairs; the lid of the mailbox kept rattling. There was no electricity so my father could not ring the doorbell. In fear she went down, and there was my father with no shoes, no socks, bloody feet, but alive and otherwise well. My mother's prayers had been heard! To this day I know it was her faith that saved my father.

From then on he had to go into hiding for fear the Germans would come and find him. We had to call him 'Aunt Annie', in case the Germans should ask us children where Papa was.

Freed by a German officer

Maria Blöte Rademaker

Our family consisted of Dad, Mom, and ten children aged four to fourteen. We lived in the northern part of Amsterdam. My sister Annie was staying with a family in Eerbeek. When that place got too dangerous during the Battle of Arnhem, my father decided to go and get her.

He didn't have a bicycle, so he set out on foot in the hope he'd be able to hitch a ride sometimes. After some days he reached Apeldoorn, where he came across some army vehicles and a fenced off area. Men and boys passing by were picked up and forced to go inside this area where they were to wait for a train that would transport them to Germany. My father was in despair, knowing he could not be spared at home. He gradually worked his way close to the fence, and, taking a photo of his family from his pocket, he tried to get the attention of a German guard. He succeeded and Dad showed him the photo. Thank God, the officer understood what Dad tried to convey. He removed him from the mass of men, and even took him to a hotel where he could stay for the night.

The next day Dad continued on his way to Eerbeek, when suddenly he heard "Halt!". This time he was stopped by two NSB guys, traitors, with their guns cocked.

"What?" said my Dad. "Yesterday I was freed by a German officer because I can't be spared at home, and now my own countrymen are going to shoot me down?

Whatever, but I'm not coming along with you."

And he kept on walking, right in front of their guns. They didn't shoot, and he arrived safely in Eerbeek.

On their way home, Dad and Annie had lots more trouble. For instance, at one point the German army vehicle in which they had hitched a ride was shot at from the skies.

We were so happy when they got back. We didn't know then that the next big trial would be the Hunger Winter.

The men were marched off

Adriana Heim-van Belle

This story is about the big razzia in Rotterdam on November 11, 1944. I was seventeen years old, and we had already been occupied for four years. I was always cold, hungry and afraid. We lived along the Rotte river.

One night I had a terrible toothache and could not sleep. There were no longer any analgesics like aspirin. My mother still had some 4711 eau de cologne which has alcohol in it, so she told me to dip my finger in that and put it on the tooth. It hurt terribly. She went back to bed and I kept sitting in a chair looking out of the window in the dark.

Gradually it became lighter and I thought I saw movement across the river, on the roof of an apartment building. By morning I saw that German soldiers were setting up machine guns. On our way to school we discovered that all the drawbridges had been pulled up and we could not cross them.

Soon vehicles with loudspeakers came through the streets, and handbills were given out at each house, ordering all men between the ages of 17 and 40 to stand out in the street, and all women to stay in the house. The men were to bring knife, fork, and cup, wear strong footwear and a warm winter coat. They were going to work for the German Wehrmacht. Anyone still found inside would be shot and their home demolished. They promised that the Wehrmacht would take care of wives and families (which never happened).

The Germans went from house to house. It was surreal and terrifying to see two soldiers in our living room. They demanded the Trouwboekje, or marriage booklet, a civil record in which all children were listed with date of birth. Although my parents had thirteen children, only three of us, all girls, still lived at home. My father was fifty-nine years old, too old, thank God.

It was so sad to see all those neighbours and boys that I had played with, standing outside in the street. Women called out of windows to their husbands and sons, crying, calling encouraging words, saying goodbye. Both ends of the street were closed off by Germans with machine guns. The men were marched off.

My mother told me to see how my oldest sister, who lived ten minutes away, had fared. Her husband had already been to Germany once, to the city of Kiel where submarines were built. He had escaped and somehow come back to Rotterdam. I set out but the Germans would not let me pass and threatened to shoot me.

Late that afternoon one of my uncles came to our house and asked to stay with us. He told us how he had escaped the razzia: a nurse living with them had some Lysol disinfectant from the hospital, so they put him to bed, he took out his dentures to make himself look even more gaunt, and then they sprinkled Lysol all over. They made a sign for the front door proclaiming typhus, for the Germans were very afraid of infectious diseases. The Germans who came to the front door refused to come in, and demanded that my brother come out. Finally they left.

I escaped in my jockey shorts

Robert Colyn

On July 10, 1944, at one in the morning, a three-man Gestapo team rang the doorbell of the Felderhof family home, where I was staying. They came to arrest me for having failed to register for the *Arbeitseinsatz*, as had been ordered back in April. In that month I had reached my 18th birthday and had decided to go into hiding after completing the school year in June. I knew that I was taking a chance of being caught before finishing the curriculum, but, in view of that possibility, had also prepared myself for a quick getaway. This over-confidence in my ability to stay a step ahead of the Nazi police almost got me caught.

I managed to escape from the house in the nick of time, while Mrs. Felderhof skillfully delayed their moving up to the second floor to search my bedroom. That short delay gave me time to move to the back of the house and slide down a drainpipe to ground level and into the back yard. From there I progressed, crouching, through some neighbouring yards in quest of a dry place to hide. There was a summer downpour all night long. I had escaped dressed only in my jockey shorts, feeling miserably cold and wet out in the open, with heavy rain pelting my body.

After waiting for about an hour, I succeeded in moving away from my street and reaching the home of one of Mrs. Felderhof's friends, Marie Schippers, who hesitantly took me in, endangering herself and her young son by doing so. Unbeknownst to me she was a member of a Resistance group in Haarlem, and had stored a number of firearms in her cellar, to be used at the time of Holland's liberation.

My narrow escape made me decide to move out of Haarlem without delay. I had to find a hiding place elsewhere, similar to that of my brother's. He had managed to hide at various places outside of Haarlem. I relocated to the east of the country, close to the German border, to a small rural town named Silvolde. I found a home with the mayor of the town, Joost Boot, whose wife, Mien, was a relative of mine.

Two months later, in September, the mayor was ordered to recruit Dutch labourers for construction of German defenses in his municipality. He refused to collaborate and went into hiding with his family and me. The three of us bicycled to Amsterdam where we separated. Nazi authorities retaliated for his sudden disappearance by burning down his house with all his belongings, and started an intensive manhunt. He and his family, however, remained safely hidden and survived the war.

From July, 1944 until the end of the war, I was unable to get any schooling and really felt like a hunted rabbit. I hid at different addresses as an 'undergrounder', as we called it, with the Gestapo snapping at my heels. In January of 1945 I experienced three narrow escapes in one day. During the third one, I escaped in female attire, with lots of face makeup, on the back of a bike ridden by a woman I had never met before. She had allowed me to enter her house while I was escaping from the Nazis during a razzia.

She offered me a hiding place in her small living room behind a hard-to-move coal stove. This very heavy iron contraption was, fortunately for me, not in use because of a lack of fuel. Right after I had twisted and folded myself behind the stove's fire screen, in a nightmarishly constricted space between the walls and the back of the stove, this lightweight woman pushed the stove back into place. Two Nazis banged on the door to demand entry to search for people in hiding. During their search I could observe them through the fine mesh of the fire screen, noting the SS insignia on their uniforms. They left, unsuccessful.

A miracle happened

Ben Wind

That last winter, 1944-'45, we had a razzia. Troops came, blocked all the roads, and went from house to house to pick up boys and men between the ages of sixteen and sixty-five. That's when a miracle happened.

An eighteen-year-old neighbour boy, who had hidden at his parents' house for more than a year, not wanting to work in Germany, came barging in. He said, "Where can I hide?" We had a small house with no place to hide. In the corner of the back room was a toilet. My mother told him to just sit there, and closed the door.

A bit later two soldiers came in and asked my dad his age. Forty. They said, "Just put on your coat and come along." After asking if there was anyone else, the soldier quickly opened the toilet door, looked in, and excused himself as he closed the door. Very likely he thought that the person with the long hair was a woman.

My Dad came home again that night, as he had the proper papers.

We buried the bicycles

Tine Steen-Dekker

In the fall of 1944, in Enkhuizen, North Holland, an order came down from the Nazi occupiers that citizens were to deliver their bicycles to the schools where the soldiers were. If not enough bicycles were delivered, serious reprisals would follow. Everyone was very frightened and sad. The Dutch used bicycles as a convenient and necessary means of transport. Every man and woman owned one.

My parents owned two sturdy, beautifully painted bicycles. They were black, with a cream-coloured line decorating the frame and mudguards, and with saddle bags. I remember my parents' fear and deliberations. Should they give up their prized possessions, necessary for life and business? What would be the consequences if they did not? Father said he had a plan, and I was to help him in the evening after dark.

That night we ate supper, and after the sun went down the windows were covered with care, as a strict blackout was enforced. We waited until the evening patrol had come and gone. Dad told me to dress warmly. We put on dark clothes, as I knew that we would be outside trying to be invisible after curfew. Father opened the back door and closed it behind us with hardly a sound. I felt like a thief. We listened for sounds of a patrol but it was dead quiet outside.

I saw Dad take one bicycle and carry it to the back fence. When he came back he handed me a large pointed spade and motioned me to follow him. He carried the other bicycle over too. The back fence had posts with sturdy chain link wire in between and a strip of wood at the top. Dad, with his long legs, could step over it. He walked to the next fence and placed the bicycles over it into a huge vegetable garden, now empty.

He took me by the hand and walked me back past our shed and through the alley between our house and the neighbours'.

"Go back now to the sidewalk and crouch down at the corner of the Vogelzang home", he whispered to me. "Look up and down the street from there, listen carefully. If you see or hear anyone coming, walk quickly here to tell me, all in a whisper. Can you do that?"

I nodded. I had done a similar job as lookout, skipping rope on the sidewalk in front of the house during the daytime, while my father was smoking undersized, and therefore illegal, eels, for our food supply. I had to watch out for Nazis coming.

After some time crouching, peeking around the corner and not seeing anything, I got bored and walked back to Father. I was sent back. This happened several times. I was asked to stick to the job. I felt lonely and was becoming cold. I waited until I had waited enough. This time my father reached over the fence and pulled me over. I watched as he threw a few spadesful of soil on a high heap which lay against a large wooden shed. He rubbed his footprints out with the shovel. I knew he had buried the bicycles in the high manure pile there.

"You mustn't tell anyone", he said.

Then, over the fences and back into our own yard. Father cleaned the shovel and stuck it in the shed's rafters. Once inside the house, we took off our boots and carried them upstairs. The living room was warm and the kettle was singing. Mother made hot water chocolate to warm us. We had no milk, as the milkman did not come around any longer. We had been given some rather chalky cocoa by the fiancé of my father's niece, a merchant marine third officer. Chalky or not, it was chocolate.

After the last Nazi soldier had left Enkhuizen, Father dug up the bicycles. I watched him carry them into the shed. They were red with rust. However, a few weeks later Father rolled out of the shed two silver-coloured bicycles.

"Why did you make them silver?" I asked, as I found it too bright and showy. Father told us that the only paint he was able to buy was silver.

Oh, those terrifying razzias!

Cornelius Zaat

Our beautiful church bells were shipped off to Germany and replaced by the rim of an old car wheel, which was banged to indicate the time of day. That sound was a direct insult to our religion and general tranquility. It was a typical example of how this so-called 'master race' preferred war machinery to the pristine sound of church bells announcing the times for worship.

Once the electricity was cut off, people had to look for alternatives. My brother Peter was a real whiz at electronics and had built several radios. So he built a 'crystal radio', which doesn't need electricity but needs a long antenna and earphones. How does one hide an antenna? For that we used a clothespin and clipped it onto the clothesline outside. It worked great.

The Germans knew that the BBC broadcast from London could be reached in occupied territory, so they installed interference noise on the particular bandwidth that the BBC broadcast used. But the British changed the bandwidth on different nights. And how did the clandestine listeners know where to find it? At about two minutes before 6 p.m. they broadcast a signal that resembled the opening bar of Beethoven's Fifth Symphony. The true meaning of it was in Morse code, the letter V, which stands for Victory.

In our house Mom and Dad's bedroom was downstairs, and just off it was a closet bed (*bedstee*), a small opening in the wall that held only a bed. That was where I slept.

In one wall there was a cubbyhole, about 20 inches wide and 16 inches high. In front of the opening was a painting of 'Christ in the Garden of Olives'. The painting hid the cubbyhole completely and it was therefore the ideal spot to hide our radio. My brothers would come into my 'bedroom' and listen to the news, often accompanied by trustworthy neighbours. I could tell by the moods of our listeners if the latest news was victory or defeat for those who fought for our freedom.

During the last year of the war, the cubbyhole became the hiding place for two of my brothers when the enemy conducted their raids. It was on these occasions that Christ in the garden of olives protected my brothers, Peter and Nico, from the intruders – I rather like this thought. How two grownup men could get themselves into this little space still makes me wonder. But they managed, and none of the boys ever got caught. My brother Aat worked at the town hall and had an excellent hiding spot there, and Gerry had his I.D. dates changed to make it appear that he was under the required age. But Mom put him in bed when the soldiers came around so he wouldn't look so tall for his age.

The worst razzia I can remember is the one that took place on December 20, 1944. It was early morning on a Catholic feast day called the Golden Mass. The mass was held very early in the morning, and during the service the word went around "Quick, hide your men!" The previous day, two of my brothers had been working in a potato field, searching for any leftover potatoes they could take home. They had used a spade and a pitchfork, but once it got dark, they had gone home, leaving their tools behind, intending to come back for them the following day.

That next day was the day of the razzia and the two potato diggers were now hiding behind Christ in the garden of olives. Dad wanted me to go to the potato field and retrieve the two valuable garden tools. I was scared, and went with leaden feet. As I was walking through the field, I heard a soldiers' truck stop on the road. The soldiers began to shout at me. I immediately dropped down and rolled myself into the nearby ditch, while I heard bullets flying by me. One of the soldiers came up to me, but when he realized that I was only an eleven-year-old kid, scared and shaking in his wooden shoes, they let me go. They did, however, take my spade and pitchfork. Dad was relieved to have me home safely, though he did mourn the loss of his garden tools.

Oh, those terrifying razzias. What went through you when you saw those trucks drive away with men you knew very well personally? And crying mothers, and wives running after them while soldiers pushed them out of the way, shaking their fists and guns at them?

"They deserve to be free"

Gertie Heinen

My parents, Roelof and Jannetje Heinen, lived in Bunschoten-Spakenburg. Spakenburg was a fishing village on the south end of the IJssel Lake. Bunschoten, a few miles to the south, was an agricultural community. My mother had been born in Spakenburg, and my father in Bunschoten. Over time, the two villages grew together into the town of Bunschoten-Spakenburg.

During the war years, Dad was involved in numerous clandestine activities: hiding young men, including my brother Arie who would otherwise have been picked up to work in Germany; butchering a pig during the night, which was highly illegal as the Germans claimed all livestock for themselves; using a milk tanker to transport banned goods; and sailing a fishing boat across the IJssel Lake with loads of potatoes. They would always make sure there was a small amount of milk near the tap in the milk tanker so that if the Germans checked up on them and opened the tap, milk would come out. The fishing boat was an old sailboat which Dad and a few other men had purchased. They gave it the name BU17.

They obtained a permit from the Germans to transport potatoes, but more often than not, other produce such as cabbages was hidden beneath the potatoes. One time there was even a slaughtered sheep. All such goods would be shared with other people.

In January of 1945, on one of their boat trips they were coming back from Friesland, an area their permit did not license them to go. Halfway back to Spakenburg they ran into a bad storm. They had to go through an area that was heavily patrolled by German boats, but they hoped the storm would keep the Germans off the water.

However, a German patrol boat must have spotted them because it set out after them. To gain speed they put up all four sails in an attempt to keep their heavily laden boat ahead of the Germans. They managed to stay ahead, but only barely. Every so often the German boat would signal them to lower their sails, but they just kept on going. Close to Spakenburg the German boat caught up, but instead of stopping them the German captain took off his hat and saluted them, and his boat left. Later they heard that the captain had been so impressed by their sailing skill with such a heavily laden boat, in such stormy weather, that he had said, "We'll let those men go. They showed such courage that they deserve to be free."

Whenever the Germans came looking for Dad at home, Mom would convince them that she had no idea where he was, and most of the time that was the truth. For Dad, the war years were one big adventure. He thrived on the danger and the challenge of outwitting the enemy.

This required retaliation

Wilhelmus Bongers

On December 30, 1944, an incident took place in De Groot's barbershop on Nieuwstraat (New Street), in Hoorn where we lived. A German officer had entered the shop for a shave and haircut. He removed his jacket and hung it on a peg, and sat down to wait his turn. In came two people from the Resistance, shot the German dead, took some papers out of the inside pocket of his jacket, and fled on foot into Kerksteeg (Church Alley) and out of sight.

This required retaliation from the Germans, of course. First the town crier was ordered to go through the city and tell the citizens that the two perpetrators had better come forward within the next few hours or the consequences would be disastrous. These two fellows left the city immediately and were nowhere to be found. At three in the afternoon of January 4, 1945, five men from a detention house in Amsterdam were led into the city by Gestapo forces, strapped onto the iron fence of the church in the church square, and each shot three times as there were three riflemen in the firing squad. We were all outside in our backyard and heard the shots very clearly, as well as the order, *"Schiessen!"* Fire!

Nelis Verbeek, the cobbler right across from the church was ordered to close his curtains and not to look out. He did as he was told but kept one window a hair's width open, and was able to see the whole thing. He told us later how awful it had been, and that he wished he had never seen it happen.

Ever since then on the 4th of May, these five men are commemorated by a quiet walk through the streets of Hoorn, following their route to the place of execution. The monument erected in one wall of the church gives their names, dates of birth, and where they had lived.

One day, while strolling along Gedempte Turfhaven (Filled Peat Harbor), a street in Hoorn, I heard a commotion across the street, right across from Ooievaar's pharmacy. A large German troop transport truck was parked there with six or eight Gestapo and SS men milling around. Their focus was on a small door between two houses, which they were trying to open.

Suddenly one of the SS men fired a shot, ran towards the door, lifted his knee-high boot and slammed it into the bottom panel of the door. It flew open, in went the Gestapo, and immediately they hauled out several women and children and at least three men. One of them, with a grey beard and wearing a hat, protested. He received a deadly kick from the boot of the same SS man, crashed down, and did not get up again. Several people witnessed this. German soldiers soon chased us away and out of sight. A few days later I went to have a closer look at that door and to see if someone had known these people who had been taken. I found no one to talk to but there was a deep gash in the door where the SS boot had done the damage. I'm told the gash is still there, many decades later.

In a wardrobe

Margaret Van Gurp

I was twelve years old when the war began. We lived in Delft, and experienced quite a lot during the war. One time the Germans came into our house to search for men. My father and brother were hiding in a large wardrobe.

I had learned German at school, so I told them that my father was dead and that I didn't have a brother. When they came into the bedrooms they found empty shells that my brother had been collecting. The Germans became very agitated, but my father and brother kept totally quiet. Luckily they weren't found.

It was a very difficult year. In early 1945 there was hardly any food, and we were always hungry and cold, because there was no heating of any kind.

Contributors

Hans Hofenk

Hans Hofenk was born in Leeuwarden, Friesland and was almost ten when the war broke out. He came to Canada in 1954, and lived in Winnipeg for five years before moving to Regina in 1960, and to Abbotsford in 2000. He worked as an engineer with Manitoba Hydro, then Saskatchewan Power. He has two children, one nearby and one in Regina. Hans still lives in Abbotsford, British Columbia, with his wife, Eva.

Jacoba Robbertsen

Jacoba Robbertsen, who was 83 in 2010 when she contributed her memories, was born in Veenendaal, Gelderland. She came to Canada in 1954, and now lives in Brampton, Ontario.

Pieter Koeleman

Pieter Koeleman was born in Noordwijk aan Zee, South Holland, where he lived during the war. He came to Canada with his wife, Beja, in 1984 to visit Pieter's brother on Quadra Island, British Columbia. On the ferry, Beja told her husband: "I want to live here!" and he agreed. The following year they moved from Holland to Campbell River, BC, with their four teenage children. One daughter returned to Holland and stayed there because she had left a boyfriend behind. The other three live near their parents and are married, with children.

Elizabeth Gilbert-de Graaff

Elizabeth Gilbert-de Graaff lives in Hampton, Virginia.

She was born in Laren, Noord Holland and was five years old when the war broke out. While studying in New York she met Les Gilbert, an American, and brought him back to Laren to get married. They returned to the USA in 1960, and lived in upstate New York where they had six children. In 1998 they moved to Hampton, Virginia, to enjoy the warmer climate there.

Afine Relk
Afine Relk was born in Bergen, North Holland, and was six when the war began. She came to the USA in 1957, shortly after marrying an American peacekeeping soldier she had met in Holland. They live in Nampa, Idaho, in potato country, with a view of the Boise Mountains. Her husband, John, still goes to the farmers market every week to sell shrubs, trees, and produce.

Tony Stroeve
Tony Stroeve escaped from occupied Holland to England in 1943, and was trained to be an RAF pilot. He survived aerial battles as a Spitfire pilot, and after Liberation learned to fly bombers in The Netherlands.

George Hansman
George Hansman was twelve years old and living in Amsterdam when the war broke out. He came to Canada with his wife and two children in 1952, settling in Dauphin, Manitoba where he worked as a mechanical engineer with CNR for the first three years. After that they moved around to far-flung places like Thunder Bay, Ontario; Corner Brook, Newfoundland, Trois Rivières, Québec, and then to Peru and Venezuela in South America. George ended his career as manager of

a paper mill. He now lives in Stevensville, Ontario, and says he still misses his work.

Maria Pais

Maria Pais was born in IJmuiden, in North Holland, and was almost twelve when the war started. She came to Philadelphia in 1951 on a scholarship to Drexel University. She studied chemical engineering, and then married her husband, Louis. His family had escaped from Holland in August of 1940 after paying a huge bribe to the Germans, permitting them to supposedly go to Mexico. Instead, they went to New York City. Louis' family was Portuguese-Jewish, and his grandparents were killed in Theresienstadt. Maria and Louis traveled all over the USA. After selling their last business in 1969, they moved to Mission Viejo, California, where Maria still lives.

Ben and Nel Meyer

Ben Meyer's story was sent in by his wife, Nel Meyer, who also sent in her own war memories. They live on Salt Spring Island, which is close to Vancouver Island, between the cities of Vancouver and Victoria.

Michael Vanderboon

Michael Vanderboon grew up in The Hague. He has been writing his family stories for several years, and is in the process of getting a longer work published. Married with 3 children and 4 grandchildren, he lives in Hidden Valley Lake, Northern California.

Corry Spruit-Degeling

Corry Spruit-Degeling was born in Hoogkarspel. She

lived in Haarlem before coming to Canada in 1957 with her husband and four children. She now lives in Calgary, Alberta.

Tom de Vries
Tom de Vries was born in Amsterdam, and came to Canada in June of 1956. He lives in Wingham, Ontario.

Henry Niezen
Henry Niezen grew up in Zwolle, in the eastern province of Overijssel. The war started when he was sixteen. He came to Canada in 1951 with his wife, two days after they got married. They had four children, in different towns, since Henry worked in construction and the family moved all over British Columbia. His four children all received a good education, and have worked as an orchestra conductor, a nurse, a professor and a forester. Henry now lives in Victoria, British Columbia.

Atty Prosper
Atty Prosper turned 90 just before sending in her story in 2010. She lives in Athens, Ontario.

Cornelis Langewis
Cornelis Langewis lived in Walnut Creek, California until his death in 2010 at the age of 92.

John van der Meer
John van der Meer was born in Indonesia, but when he was one year old his family moved to Holland. He came to Canada with his wife, Johanna. They lived in Nanaimo, British Columbia until his death early in 2012.

Henk van der Meulen

Henk van der Meulen, who sent in a story told by his Aunt Dinie, lives in Burlington, Ontario. His Aunt Dinie died in March of 2011.

Karel Stuut

Karel Stuut grew up in Haarlem, and now lives in Dollard des Ormeaux, Québec.

Yvonne Harvey Shea

Yvonne Harvey Shea makes her home in Stanwood, Washington.

Bouk Jobsis

Bouk Jobsis , before coming to the USA in 1964, lived in The Netherlands, where she worked as a midwife – she delivered more than 200 babies – and in Iran. She settled in Houston Texas after a year in Utah. Bouk has two daughters.

Susan Rombeek

Susan Rombeek grew up in The Hague. She moved to Washington in 1967 with her husband, Edward. In fact, on the day he was discharged from the Dutch Navy, they headed for their ship, the Rijndam. Susan sold yard goods in a department store before returning to university to get her Master's degree in counseling psychology. She then worked as a school psychologist. She lives on Guemes Island, near Anacortes, Washington.

Anne Hendren

Anne Hendren was twelve years old when the war broke out, and lived in Utrecht.

She now lives in Salem, Oregon.

Catherina de Leeuw
Catherina de Leeuw was born in The Hague and was seven when the war started. In 1958 she came to Canada with her husband, and settled in Wallaceburg, Ontario where they had five children. She contributed her war story from Chatham, Ontario. She still keeps busy with church work, quilting, and grandchildren, among other things.

Schelte (Sam) Brandsma
Schelte (Sam) Brandsma grew up on a farm in the north of Friesland. He and his wife came to Canada in 1951 as newlyweds, with the boat trip serving as their honeymoon. They had five boys and two girls, and now have fourteen grandchildren.

Schelte has lived in Lindsay, Ontario, since 1952, while spending the first year on a farm, which was a requirement for most new immigrants at the time. His wife died in 2006.

Doortje Shover
Doortje Shover's younger years were spent in Rotterdam.

Maria Blöte-Rademaker
Maria Blöte-Rademaker lives in Cobble Hill, British Columbia.

Adriana Heim-van Belle
Adriana Heim-van Belle's childhood home was in Rotterdam.
She now lives in North Las Vegas, Nevada.

Robert Colyn

Robert Colyn was fourteen when the war began. He lived in a boarding house in Haarlem while going to school. His parents were stationed in the Dutch East Indies, and were interned in Japanese camps. He did not see them from 1939 until after the war. Robert moved to Brazil with his wife in 1951, and then lived in Akron, Ohio until 1962. After four years in The Netherlands, he moved to Salinas, California, where he still lives.

Ben Wind

Ben Wind lives in Vancouver, British Columbia.

Tine Steen-Dekker

Tine Steen-Dekker lived in Enkhuizen, North Holland, during the war. She makes her home in Edmonton, Alberta.

Cornelius Zaat

Cornelius (Con) Zaat was born in 1933 in the village of Kwintsheul, in the province of South Holland, where he grew up. During the early 1950s the Canadian forces were advertising in Dutch music magazines for musicians to help build up military bands across the country. Con's brother signed up first, and Con followed a year later, coming to Prince Edward Island in 1955. He played clarinet, bassoon, saxophone, and several other instruments. He later taught music in the schools and played in the Island's symphony orchestra in his spare time. Con's civic marriage had taken place before he left Holland, but his wife was not able to come to Canada until five months later, at which time the marriage was blessed in the church. Con and his wife consider that their 'real' marriage date. He continues to live in Montague, Prince Edward Island.

Gertie Heinen
Gertie Heinen comes from Bunschoten, a small fishing village near Holland's large inland sea, IJssel Lake. She now lives in Picture Butte, Alberta

Wilhelmus Bongers
Wilhelmus (Bill) Bongers, now deceased, was born in 1933. He grew up in Hoorn, in the province of North Holland. In Canada, he married a French-Canadian and worked for Nortel for many years. After their retirement Bill and his wife made their home in Bathurst, New Brunswick.

Margaret van Gurp
Margaret Van Gurp sent her contribution to this book from Halifax, Nova Scotia.

The Dutch in Wartime series

Book 1
Invasion

Edited by:
Tom Bijvoet

90 pages paperback
ISBN: 978-0-9868308-0-8

Book 2
Under Nazi Rule

Edited by:
Tom Bijvoet

88 pages paperback
ISBN: 978-0-9868308-3-9

Book 3
Witnessing the Holocaust

Edited by:
Tom Bijvoet

96 pages paperback
ISBN: 978-0-9868308-5-3

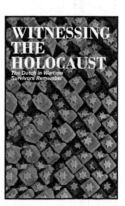

Book 4
Resisting Nazi Occupation

Edited by:
Anne van Arragon Hutten

108 pages paperback
ISBN: 978-0-9868308-4-6

Book 5
Tell your children about us

Edited by:
Anne van Arragon Hutten

104 pages paperback
ISBN: 978-0-9868308-6-0

Book 6
War in the Indies

Edited by:
Anne van Arragon Hutten

96 pages paperback
ISBN: 978-0-9868308-7-7

Book 7
Caught in the crossfire

Edited by:
Anne van Arragon Hutten

104 pages paperback
ISBN: 978-0-9868308-8-4

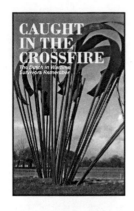

Book 8
The Hunger Winter

Edited by:
Tom Bijvoet &
Anne van Arragon Hutten

110 pages paperback
ISBN: 978-0-9868308-9-1

Book 9
Liberation

Editcd by:
Anne van Arragon Hutten

114 pages paperback
ISBN: 978-0-9919981-0-4

*Keep your series complete: order on-line at
mokeham.com or contact Mokeham Publishing.*